DAVID SHIRREFF

$

BREAK ·······► UP

MELVILLE HOUSE
BROOKLYN · LONDON

THE BANKS!

A PRACTICAL GUIDE TO
STOPPING THE NEXT GLOBAL
FINANCIAL MELTDOWN

BREAK UP THE BANKS!

First Melville House Printing: March 2016

Melville House Publishing   8 Blackstock Mews
46 John Street   and   Islington
Brooklyn, NY 11201   London N4 2BT

mhpbooks.com   facebook.com/mhpbooks   @melvillehouse

Library of Congress Cataloging-in-Publication Data
Names: Shirreff, David, 1947– author.
Title: Break up the banks! : a practical guide to stopping the next
global financial meltdown / David Shirreff.
Description: Brooklyn, NY : Melville House, [2016]
Identifiers: LCCN 2016003709| ISBN 9781612195025 (paperback) |
ISBN 9781612195032 (ebook)
Subjects: LCSH: Banks and banking—Government policy. |
Financial institutions—Government policy. | Financial crises—
Prevention. | BISAC: BUSINESS & ECONOMICS / Banks &
Banking. | POLITICAL SCIENCE / Public Policy / Economic
Policy. | POLITICAL SCIENCE / Economic Conditions.
Classification: LCC HG1573 .S535 2016 | DDC 332.1—dc23
LC record available at http://lccn.loc.gov/2016003709

Design by Marina Drukman

Printed in the United States of America
10   9   8   7   6   5   4   3   2   1

When the capital development of a country becomes a by-product of the activities of a casino, the job is likely to be ill-done.

—JOHN MAYNARD KEYNES,
The General Theory of Employment, Interest and Money

CONTENTS

THE NEED FOR MORE RADICAL REFORM

This is a call for revolution—a revolution to reduce complexity in global banks, to split them into manageable chunks, and to change the self-serving nature of the culture that dominates them.

These recommendations are not plucked out of the blue. They represent a reasonable course of action, given the mess that finance has gotten itself into over the past two decades. That mess is the subject of the first part of this book. There have, of course, been many accounts of the origins of the 2008 financial crisis, but I'd argue that it's a story that can't be retold too many times. To understand where to go, we first have to understand how it is that we got here.

Most of the remedies that I offer in the second part of this book have already been hinted at, sporadically, by many commentators, but usually without being fashioned into a coherent plan. In the years since the initial, post-crisis burst of enthusiasm, financial-sector and banking reform has lost its way, though it seems to be stumbling, half-blind, toward the solutions you find here. This is an attempt to speed up that process.

Before the financial crisis, discussions of financial reform were inevitably marginal; there was no crisis, so public awareness of the issues was limited. Financial reform was technical, its real-world consequences little understood.

But since 2008, reform has—belatedly—become a topic of widespread attention. What was once the province of academic articles and the occasional op-ed column is now mainstream. The United States, the United Kingdom, and Europe have tussled with reform over the past few years with varying degrees of ambition, earnestness, and efficacy, but no one thinks we've seen the end of it. (Other than bankers—but then, everyone's entitled to his fantasies.)

This is not a radical book. At least, it shouldn't be: *Break Up the Banks!* is concerned with pragmatic ideas—not punitive or utopian ones. Still, for many, the measures that I am proposing might appear somehow beyond the pale. What I would argue, in response, is that fear of being radical has led to the situation we are in today.

Since 2008, an extraordinary amount of money has been devoted to recapitalizing and strengthening bank balance sheets in the interest of protecting the financial system—and thus the global economy. But the effect of this investment has been to sustain a sector that is still failing to serve the real economy efficiently. Instead of the banking and financial sectors being reformed to serve the real economy, much of the value added by the real economy is still being hoovered up by the banking system. This approach—and the assumptions that bolster it—has to change. I hope that *Break Up the Banks!* can contribute to that change.

Part One

WHAT WENT WRONG?

1

MISSION CREEP

Big Bang and the Lifting of Glass-Steagall

Banks have always been dangerous, and thus have always been bound by rules and regulations of varying degrees of intensity. A bank, after all, is nothing without the laws that allow it to exist. But in the 1980s and '90s, laws that governed the scope and scale of banks were substantially liberalized. This liberalization happened in a number of other industries (the landscape of American airlines before and after the late 1970s is a good example of how dramatic these changes were), but the impact on banking was probably the most consequential in terms of global politics and the structure of society. In a rather short span, many of the laws that had kept banks from becoming too big and too dominant (and thus too dangerous) were deemed outmoded. Deregulation was in.

In Britain, the turning point was Big Bang. On October 27, 1986, banks were allowed to deal directly in securities and on the London Stock Exchange. Suddenly, banks based in Britain could provide all types of financial services to a broad range of clients. And stockbrokers and stockjobbers (market makers in securities)—which had been kept strictly separate—could now be bought by and integrated into banks that would soon grow bigger than ever.

In the United States, the 1999 Gramm-Leach-Bliley Act effectively repealed the Glass-Steagall Act of 1933, which had enforced the separation of investment banking from commercial banking activity. Glass-Steagall was hugely important: it was nothing less than America's answer to the near-failure of the financial system. Gramm-Leach-Bliley was equally important, but in the inverse. It paved the way for giant "universal" banks that could use the stability of their retail deposits to take bigger and bigger bets on the wholesale credit, securities, and derivatives markets. That turned out to be a recipe for disaster.

Financial Engineering: Useful Instruments Become Self-Serving

In their early days, financial derivatives—products whose value is determined by the variation in price of a traded item—served a real purpose as an insurance or source of protection against future price movements. For instance, trading of interest-rate futures on the Chicago Mercantile Exchange and the invention of interest-rate and currency swaps met a genuine customer need. These products offered simple solutions to complex financial problems.

Swaps, to take one example, replaced complex back-to-back loans made by pairs of companies in different currencies or different markets: an American company wanting a source of Japanese yen could "swap" its own fixed-rate debt in dollars for a Japanese company's floating-rate debt in yen. The companies could then settle the difference in each other's obligations without the extra trouble and expense of raising finance in a foreign currency in which they were not well-known borrowers. Once swaps caught on, they greatly widened companies' access to finance in different markets.

But by the 1990s, the rewards that arrangers could earn for being the first to create a more and more complex financial product were simply too tempting. This put a premium on complexity and opacity. Perhaps the apogee of this era was the creation of the "quanto" swap—nothing more than a bet on the future difference between short-term and long-term interest rates in a pair of currencies and the exchange-rate risk between them. The quanto swap had no conceivable economic relevance for the buyer.

Libor Squared was another—a swap based not on a simple interest rate, Libor, but on its square. Libor Squared amplified modest changes in the rate and increased risk and volatility. This might have been clever, but again, what was the point? What was the economic purpose of such a transaction?

In the post-deregulation age, these audacious but pointless tricks became the norm, rather than the exception.

Fear of Currency and Interest-Rate Volatility and Illiquidity

With the explosion in trading, a succession of exchange-rate and interest-rate shocks during the 1980s and '90s, and increased globalization, there was an inevitable tendency toward short-termism and the desire to protect oneself from price volatility. It became increasingly important for financial positions to be tradable. Above all, traders wanted financial instruments that were liq-

uid—quickly sellable for cash. And that view affected the behavior of corporate treasurers and investors: short-term financial
gains became a more important focus for them than a company's
long-term strategy. It was a phenomenon that fed on itself, to the
detriment of the underlying economy.

The Bloating of the Financial Sector and the Quest
for Economies of Scale

As a result of the plethora of new instruments and new financial-
engineering techniques, the turnover of the financial services sector naturally grew—as did the share of financial services in the
United States and UK GDP. And the companies themselves grew,
as well. JPMorgan Chase and Bank of America now have gross
assets of over $2 trillion *each*, while Barclays and Deutsche Bank
are not far behind with assets of around $1.8 trillion. However
meaningless those numbers may be, they indicate a huge volume
and mix of businesses that is a challenge to manage in good times,
let alone at a time of crisis. After all, the assets of Lehman Brothers
were "only" around $640 billion at the time of its collapse in 2008,
and the process of closing the bank down—known as the windup
process—has been going on for seven years and counting.

And it is not just the balance sheet. Deutsche Bank is not
one single entity. It comprises more than 1,000 separate units,
including 376 subsidiaries, 394 special-purpose vehicles, and 406
significant equity holdings, according to its annual report. In my
opinion, there is no "optimal" size for a bank—but a bank with
a balance sheet of $500 billion (or perhaps even $250 billion) is

almost certainly too big, either because of market domination or complexity.

In a 2012 speech on banks' economies of scale, Andy Haldane, executive director of the Bank of England, made an important, related point. He said that the lower funding costs enjoyed by banks that are "too big to fail" (i.e., so big that the government would rather rescue them than risk the economic shock of their failure) seem to be the reason why economies of scale at big banks with assets of more than $100 billion continue to improve with size. Take away this funding advantage, he went on, and there is no evidence that bigger banks are more efficient than small ones.

The Ascent of Credit Modeling

As finance became more and more complex, as banks became bigger, and as quantitative finance took on a life of its own, financial engineers began to think that credit risk might be just as tradable as interest-rate, currency, and equity-index risk had become. They developed models that took the average performance of a bundle of loans, and used that as a proxy to predict the behavior of a portfolio of similar loans. In theory this would save them the bother of having to assess individual credits and would achieve economies of scale. Such bundling works well for certain types of credit, such as consumer debt, mortgages, or car loans, where customer behavior is broadly consistent and has a long data history. But it is dangerous to apply it to company loans, where default rates are less predictable.

Unfortunately, the financial engineers were more keen to

apply their credit risk models to company loans, where the big money is. They invented credit default swaps (CDSs), a form of insurance against the event of a company defaulting on its debt. And they also came up with collateralized debt obligations (CDOs)—bundles of credits that could be sliced and diced to meet a particular investor's alleged appetite for risk. And then they convinced the rating agencies to put their stamp of approval on the creditworthiness of each part of the bundle.

Regulators tried to squash this early in the game, but they failed. Banks were soon using their own models of credit risk to show regulators that they had a better grasp of the overall risk on their loan portfolio. They finally managed to persuade them that this new understanding should allow them to reduce the amount of capital held against the risk of the loans going bad.

Regulatory Capture, Regulatory Complexity

Since the 1988 Basel Accord, or Basel I, bank regulators have led a merry dance trying to devise rules that constrain what complex banks are doing. But again and again, they've been stymied by what's known as regulatory capture. The journalist David Sirota has written that the term "shrouds a serious problem in vaguely academic jargon," but in short, it refers to the ease with which officials move back and forth between big banks and the institutions that are meant to regulate them. If the "revolving door" usually describes a politician's path to lobbying and back again (or vice versa), regulatory capture homes in more specifically on the agencies that try to limit banks' questionable behaviors.

In part as a result of regulatory capture, banking rulemakers have ended up allowing almost every form of financial innovation—good or bad—but worst of all, they handed over risk measurement to the banks themselves, allowing banks to use their own "models" to calculate their own regulatory capital requirements. It's not hard to see why banks aren't necessarily best qualified to assess their own trouble spots.

Over the years, the Basel Committee on Banking Supervision has produced thicker and thicker volumes on bank capital requirements—which have required bigger and bigger compliance departments to administer. But even so, ever since the principle was conceded that banks set the pace, supervisors have been stumbling to catch up.

The most egregious example of this was the treatment of credit-risk modeling. In September 1998, at a conference sponsored by the Bank of England, various credit-risk models were paraded before regulators and found wanting. As a result, a decision was taken not to allow credit-risk modeling as part of banks' calculations on the amount of capital they must hold under the pending Basel rules known as Basel II. That was then.

Within a year or two, with the development of a market in credit default swaps, the use of credit-risk modeling had become widespread—and the game was up. The regulators had been finessed, and the notion that credit risk could be hedged by means of credit default swaps was included (and explicitly recognized) in Basel II.

And Basel III, which is now being implemented (admittedly sporadically) in various jurisdictions, is a testament to the seemingly infinite expansion of complexity. Additional rules for liquidity and the demand for "living wills"—blueprints for the orderly windup of a bank—have added to the regulatory and compliance burden, not just for banks, but for regulators, too.

Basel IV, if bank regulators pursue the Basel route, is likely to be even more complex.

The Gaming of Risk-Weighted Assets

Allowing banks to use their own view of risk as a regulatory benchmark is fraught with problems. In particular, highly leveraged investment banks have been able to present a less frightening picture of themselves by using the concept of risk-weighted assets (RWAs). These banks assign a measure of riskiness to all of their assets using their home-grown models of how risky each asset is—in terms of credit risk, market risk, or any other kind of unpredictability It's through this kind of clever assessment that Barclays' gross assets at the end of September 2015 could be reduced from £1,237 billion to RWAs totaling a mere £382 billion. With RWAs, anything is possible.

Unfortunately, such measures are meaningless without detailed knowledge of how that reduction was made—and that is seldom obvious. But one thing has become clearer since the crisis: the leverage ratio—the relationship between a bank's gross assets and the size of its capital buffer (the mandatory capital a financial institution is required to hold)—is a far more important and robust indicator. The RWA figure may give some comfort day-to-day, but in times of stress it will not count for much; it is the gross figure on which a bank lives or dies. For years, the U.S. Federal Deposit Insurance Corporation (FDIC) fought to retain the use of the leverage ratio while more liberal regulators thought it passé. Now, the leverage ratio is back in fashion, precisely because it is so hard to game. That's a kind of progress, however modest.

Superabundance of Liquidity

The easy availability of cheap debt, reinforced by banks' ability to securitize assets and get them off the balance sheet (at least in theory), led to a massive expansion of credit from Seattle to Saloniki in the years before the crisis. Low interest rates in the euro zone intensified the effect in countries such as Ireland, Spain, and Greece.

In the United States, the combination of easy credit and securitization amplified a housing bubble that, when it burst (as bubbles usually do), triggered the financial crisis from which we all suffered. With hindsight, a credit bubble in one sector or another, inflated by securitization, would probably have burst in Europe or America sooner or later anyway. But the fact is that the housing bubble in the United States signaled the start of the crisis.

The Rating Agencies

Still, whether or not the bursting of the bubble was inevitable, there is plenty of blame to go round.

In particular, many people have pointed the finger at the

credit rating agencies. Certainly, the three biggest (Moody's, Standard & Poor's, and Fitch) allowed themselves to be drawn into a new and expanding source of income, rating tranches of "structured" securitized assets, such as CDOs.

This was unknown territory for them, since it involved not only rating the aggregate credit risk of each tranche, but also the quality of the CDO "manager"—the individual or firm entrusted with buying and selling assets in the asset pool—who could fine-tune the pool by trading the assets. In other words, these were no longer simple corporate credit risks, but highly complex animals with a life of their own—a characteristic largely, if not totally, ignored by rating agencies, investors, and regulators until it was too late.

Despite the continued difficulty of rating these tranches of securities, the rating agencies are still being asked to provide this service. A rating from one or more of the three agencies is still a requirement for most institutional investments in publicly traded instruments. And there is a continued conflict of interest, because these rating agencies are usually paid for their services by the issuer of the securities. This relatively new line of business, dented by the crisis, is making a comeback, and is a continuing source of revenue—and conflict of interest—for the three usual suspects.

Unfortunately, there is no obvious alternative. Other rating agencies have tried to compete, but the experience of Fitch, the youngest of the big three, suggests that it takes years to break into the oligopoly.

Egan Jones, a Pennsylvania-based rater of corporate bonds, has tried to do so—with limited success. So has Jules Kroll, who made his reputation in the spooky world of financial investigation. More recently, Scope, a Berlin-based rater of investment funds, has turned its attention to rating European banks. At least two of these charge investors, rather than issuers, for their services—which takes care of one potential conflict. But it is likely to be years before ratings from any of these agencies are interchangeable with those of the established three.

Arrogance and Entitlement: The New Breed of Banker

Partners who harness their personal wealth to the fortunes of a financial institution with unlimited liability can, with some justification, pay themselves as much of the proceeds as they think the firm can bear. This was how it worked in the 1970s and '80s: Wall Street investment banking partnerships would scoop half of the firm's revenues into a bonus pool, from which they would reward themselves and their staff. Some years, they did extraordinarily well; in other years, partners ate losses to keep the show on the road. It was not perfect—bankers still occasionally bet the ranch and lost—but the losses were borne by themselves and their creditors—not the taxpayer.

But when those financial institutions changed their status to joint-stock or publicly listed companies—as most of them did—they should have changed their remuneration practices. Employees of post-deregulation banks may be shareholders, but they can't be partners: the most they can lose (apart from their job) is their stake in the company. And because of their comparatively limited exposure, they shouldn't be entitled to treat the firm as their personal pocketbook, as partners did in the past. It's a matter of skin in the game, to use a phrase often misattributed to Warren Buffett.

Unfortunately, the culture of entitlement that characterized the partnership structure survived the change of ownership. Worse, the same culture was picked up by commercial banks that wanted to break into investment banking. In order to lure top investment bankers, they believed that they had to offer the same kind of deal—or in some cases even more, with bonuses guaranteed for several years. The rules of the game were skewed unfairly in these employees' favor at a most dangerous time for the banking sector.

Increasingly, bankers were led to believe that they were masters of the universe, creating value where there was none before. They felt it appropriate to reward themselves out of bonus pools that generally raked off 50 percent of the revenue (that's revenue, not profit) generated by the sale of risky structured-debt products. Since the credit risk involved did not go away, they had unwittingly (or, worse still, wittingly) *increased* the risk of loss for their customers.

Note that there was no question of individual bankers sharing the pain of loss. Their business model allowed them to take a share of the upside, while leaving the downside for others to bear.

Regulators and governments have, from time to time, tried to address this "agency" problem by ordering the deferral and possible clawback of bonuses over a three- to ten-year period. That may have modified the bankers' sense of entitlement—but it hasn't eliminated it.

It should be said—though perhaps it doesn't need to be—
that this sense of entitlement among financial sector employees is unique. Workers in other sectors, such as retail, health
care, construction, etc., do not demand the same conditions or
benefits, though the social utility of their labor isn't any less
significant. In the 1980s, investment bankers' pay was roughly
equivalent to that of other professionals; by 2007, the aforemen-
tioned sense of entitlement had caused it to grow to nearly four
times as much.

The special treatment enjoyed by financial intermediaries
has been self-perpetuating. Those who could, in theory, set limits on banker compensation are often on a similar gravy train:
they include employees at institutional shareholders, such as
managers of pension funds and insurance companies; corporate
executives; compensation consultants; regulators (some of whom
might have an eye on a job in the private sector—the lure of
regulatory capture); and analysts at banks and rating agencies.
None of them has been particularly critical of such levels of compensation—nor have most politicians and government officials,
who may also be looking at the revolving door.

And the industry itself—along with its well-remunerated
spin doctors—has been immensely successful at convincing deci-
sion-makers that it would be dangerous to interfere with the way
banks handle compensation. "Talent," it's declared ominously,
might flee abroad or into other sectors, leaving finance to be run
by the second-rate, though the likelihood of this outcome seems
highly doubtful. Even the most recent efforts to cap bonuses have
not attempted or dared to address the entrenched principle of
entitlement.

Interconnectedness

In the quest to trade higher and higher volumes, financial institutions found ways of shunting liquidity between each other that were almost frictionless. Very little account was taken of what it might mean for a number of different firms to be so exposed to each other at a time of crisis and panic. It was like a giant game of hot potato—except that there were many hot potatoes, and almost everyone had one in his hands already.

After Lehman Brothers collapsed, the general consensus was that the system could not afford to let other big firms go down. The result was, for example, that the insurance company AIG was bailed out. Why? Because its financial products division was believed to be interconnected with almost all of the other big investment-banking groups. Each one of those groups, and those groups' creditors in turn, would have faced an unknown black hole in its balance sheet if AIG had been allowed to go under. It was widely feared that the developed world's financial system, which was already traumatized, would grind to a halt.

Maybe that was true. Maybe governments really did have no choice.

The interbank lending market—in which banks lend to each other short-term without posting collateral—was the first casualty of the trauma. First central banks, and then governments, had to step in to fill the gap in liquidity provision, which meant that they made it easy for banks to raise emergency funding, by letting them pawn almost any dubious loans and other assets at the central bank, for ready cash.

That situation has not changed much, even though the crisis

has abated. Even today, banks are refinancing more through central banks than they are with other entities in the market. It may be that the interbank market will never reach its former volume, and that's probably a good thing: interbank lending is a convenient way for banks to manage their liquidity, but it has proved highly sensitive to contagion as soon as there is any concern about the creditworthiness of a bank or group of banks. Far better, in my opinion, that banks should find other sources of liquidity—though perhaps not just from central banks.

Despite the demise of the interbank market, banks are still left with huge volumes of bilateral positions with each other, particularly in nonstandard swaps and derivatives. Which means that interconnectedness remains a problem: the next time a bank finds itself in trouble, the consequences will again extend beyond—perhaps far beyond—the source of the problem.

Holding Governments to Ransom

In the financial crisis that began in 2008, domestic governments in America, Britain, Ireland, Iceland, Germany, France, Italy, Austria, and so on were forced to intervene. In most cases, banks were recapitalized by the governments' purchase of shares in the institutions. Yet only in a very few cases were banks actually nationalized.

In America, the situation was rather different. Those banks deemed to be "systemic" were forced to take on $10 billion of government capital, and broker-dealers like Goldman Sachs and Morgan Stanley were forced (and/or persuaded) to become regulated banks, with access to the Federal Reserve's discount window. The newly elected President Barack Obama also announced a temporary cap of $500,000 on top executive pay, though that cap proved so temporary as to be essentially nonexistent. According to a 2012 article in *The New York Times*, in response to a report that salaries often remained enormous, the U.S. Department of the Treasury "noted that the $500,000 cap on salaries was merely a guideline, not a provision of law or a regulation." Even under the cap, stock awards and other goodies took overall pay for many well over the $500,000 mark. In mid-2009, JPMorgan Chase, Goldman Sachs, Morgan Stanley, and others were allowed to repay their $10 billion of government rescue capital, and were able to escape the cap. By December 2009, Citigroup and Bank of America had also managed to repay and escaped the cap from 2010 onward. So nothing has changed. (In their compensation for 2015, the bosses of JPMorgan, Goldman Sachs, and Morgan Stanley each notched up more than $20 million.)

And in Britain, the government was even more timid. Although two big banks, the Royal Bank of Scotland and Lloyds Banking Group, became respectively 87 percent and 43 percent government-owned, those share holdings were delegated to UK Financial Investments. Although UKFI was an agency within the Treasury, its officials were rather hesitant to influence the banks, particularly on pay. Their reticence reflected their belief that the banks should be returned to wider share ownership as soon as possible. The timidity and ineffectiveness of UKFI persist today.

Quantitative Easing

A mantra during the crisis, endlessly repeated by Ben Bernanke, chairman of the U.S. Federal Reserve, was the need to use aggressive monetary policy to keep the economy from falling into recession or depression. The method used, in both Britain and the United States, was quantitative easing (QE), whereby the central bank buys assets with its own money. The theory goes that these purchases help lower the price of credit and make credit more accessible to parts of the economy where there is demand.

In its pursuit of QE, the Fed bought a range of assets, including Treasury bonds, agency bonds (bonds backed by a government agency), and agency mortgage-backed securities. That offered direct financial assistance to American nonbank companies. Under Britain's version of QE, the UK Treasury's instruction to the Bank of England allowed it to buy corporate assets as well as gilts (UK treasury bonds). In practice, however, the Bank concentrated almost entirely on buying gilts, which had the effect of pumping cheap finance into the financial system, but not the real economy. As a result, British QE had little direct effect on nonfinancial companies.

The big unknown is whether QE—and the resulting very low interest rates—has done much more than push investments into stock markets, in the search for higher returns, and drive up the price of equities. And the conundrum for the Fed and the Bank of England remains: How does one get the country off the drug of QE without sending the domestic economy (and, in the case of the dollar, emerging markets as well) into a tailspin? The worldwide disarray in stock markets that followed the

Fed's 0.25 percent hike in interest rates on December 16, 2015, showed how difficult it would be to wean the world off QE.

The Euro-Zone Crisis as Destroyer of Government/Bank Symbiosis

Once euro-zone governments had rescued their banks (and apparently stabilized the financial system), creditors began to turn their fire on to the governments standing behind those banks. If the banks' capital consisted mainly of their home nation's government bonds, then, inevitably, they could be no more secure than the governments standing behind them.

In time, it became clear that there could be no real return of confidence unless the euro-zone banks were seen as stable according to a common trans-euro-zone benchmark. The idea of a banking union was born—with the goal of a common supervisor (single supervisory mechanism—SSM—under the European Central Bank), a single resolution mechanism (SRM), and a single rulebook.

But the conundrum remains: To prevent a total collapse of confidence in the banks of some euro-zone countries, their portfolios of home-country government bonds continue to be counted as risk-free, i.e., having a zero weighting among their risk-weighted assets. This is the case even in the latest version of the Basel rulebook, implemented in the EU as CRD 4, at least for banks which do not (or choose not to) use internal risk models to set regulatory capital.

This fudge may be necessary in the short term. After all,

where else would governments place their unwanted bonds than with their own banks—which can then post them as collateral for cash with the European System of Central Banks?

But it remains to be seen how long a Europe-wide banking system can live with such a fudge. Thomas Mayer, formerly chief economist for Deutsche Bank, has suggested the problem could be sanitized if euro-zone banks exchanged their national sovereign bonds for bonds issued by the European Central Bank, guaranteed by all euro-zone states. But offering such a guarantee is anathema to major euro-zone governments, especially Germany, whose chancellor Angela Merkel said, when the subject was raised in 2012, "Not in my lifetime."

2

HALFHEARTED FIXES

Many of the weaknesses in the post-crisis banking and financial system have been addressed over the past few years. But it is far from clear that these reforms have created, or will ever create, a financial system that is both safer and a better servant of the real economy.

In the United States, the Dodd-Frank Act of 2010 was more than nothing—far more, if you listen to the voices in certain quarters. But no one can dispute that in its final form, the law is considerably less ambitious and effective than it was when it was proposed (as laws usually are before the lobbyists get to them). I'll discuss some of these limitations below, but suffice it to say here that Dodd-Frank's greatest weakness is the weakened interpretation of the so-called Volcker Rule, which was meant to outlaw proprietary trading at banks.

In Europe, various high-level commissions have produced recommendations on how the banking and financial sector might be restructured—notably the Independent Commission on Banking (known as the Vickers Commission) in Britain, and the High-Level Expert Group on reforming the structure of the EU banking sector (known as the Liikanen Group). These have resulted in bank reform legislation in Britain, Germany, and France and a new framework proposed by the European Commission in January 2014. But a lot of the sharpness of the original recommendations has been lost.

It is worth reviewing what is going on, and where—if only to explode the notion that the authorities have everything under control, and that we have no need to worry anymore about the safety and soundness of the global financial system.

Raising Banking Standards

Let's start with the banks themselves. Naturally, the industry is not exactly thrilled at the prospect of radical reform—though when prodded, it tends to concede that something must be done. Still, in the United States, it's hard to find anything other than total opposition to any kind of initiatives—even from lobbyists from banks that owe their entire continued existence to government intervention.

Among their British counterparts, things look a little better. The UK financial industry's approach has been incremental—and essentially voluntary. In September 2013, Britain's five biggest banks announced that they would fund an independent banking standards body—a body which is emphatically intended not to be just another bank lobby group. This was in response to calls by the Commission on Banking Standards for a "unified professional body" to be set up, without subsidy, to establish higher standards in the sector. "The body must never allow itself to become a cozy sinecure for retired bank chairmen and City grandees," cautioned the parliamentary report.

The body may help to make bankers more aware of their duties toward their customers, but the likelihood that it will prompt radical change in UK banking is quite small. Any hopes that the official regulator might get tougher on this point were dashed in December 2015, when the Financial Conduct Authority shelved plans for a much-feared inquiry into bank culture. The Conservative government, well into its second term in power, seemed to have decided that "banker-bashing" must stop.

UK Banking Reform Act

Legislation that started tough when the Banking Reform Act was passed in 2013 is getting weaker by the day. The accompanying regulations are still being haggled over by the banks and the Bank of England, though they still include some of the Vickers reforms. So what about reform in the UK that's not led by the industry? Well, there are some modest bright spots.

In particular, they deal with the issue of ring-fencing—the separation of a bank's retail operations from other parts of the bank, without a complete legal separation. That said, according to the legislation, small banks (those with core deposits below £25 billion) are exempt from ring-fencing, and certain customers— large organizations and sophisticated private investors—may make deposits with the non-ring-fenced part of the bank.

As it stands, the ring-fenced entities will still be able to deal with:

- simple derivatives (up to a threshold amount)
- securitization of their own assets
- debt-equity swaps
- certain "ancillary" activities

That's quite a big loophole, though they will be prohibited from having exposures to:

- other banks (except for other ring-fenced banks)
- investment firms (except those not authorized to deal in investments as principal or as agent)
- insurers (including reinsurers and insurance holding companies)
- investment funds and fund management firms
- securitization companies
- financial holding companies

Another loophole: they will be allowed to take trade-finance exposures to foreign banks. And they will be able to hedge themselves against default risk that they own. In other words, even ring-fenced banks are going to be doing some pretty fancy stuff; it is not just meat-and-potatoes "narrow" banking. Moreover, ongoing consultations suggest that the firewall between the ring-fenced entity and the parent group will be wafer-thin, especially regarding a group's ability to shunt spare capital across the fence. The British Bankers Association has argued that banks in Britain would otherwise be heading for a competitive disadvantage. Expect more dilution before the ring-fence finally comes into force in 2019.

The impact assessment attached to the legislation makes the bold prediction that the Banking Reform Act will produce a net benefit to the UK economy (because of added stability and the reduced severity of a future crisis) of £114 billion over the next thirty years—bravo! Excuse me if I don't get too excited.

Other initiatives are unlikely to have much impact. In June 2013, for instance, the UK Parliamentary Commission on Banking Standards (chaired by Andrew Tyrie MP) made its own contribution—a barrage of conflicting recommendations in a report called *Changing Banking for Good*.

Among them was a break-up of RBS into regional and business units—although the Commission also suggested a split into a "good" bank (or banks) and a "bad" bank (which would remain in government ownership). These suggestions are useful, but, in my opinion, they have confused preserving value for the taxpayer with preserving value for remaining shareholders. We need to take a more radical approach. UK banking reform is stymied, to some extent, by the pressure for harmonized financial regulation across the European Union. British ring-fencing is in principle tougher than EU plans to segregate commercial and investment banking. But the fear of being left with a competitive disadvantage is spurring these regulatory initiatives in a race to the bottom. The opportunity for radical reform offered by the crisis has been more or less squandered. Is there any country that has truly seized the moment?

Big American Banks, Weakened Dodd-Frank

Not, unfortunately, in the United States. The United States is not exactly a shining light for reform, and indeed, in at least one important way, it is heading in precisely the wrong direction.

America's banking assets are not as disproportionately large in relation to GDP as those, for example, in Britain, the Netherlands, Switzerland, or even Germany. But, since the crisis, the biggest U.S. banks have been growing, not shrinking. And that is not making them any easier to manage or regulate. JPMorgan Chase, for example, has clearly become an unwieldy conglomerate of franchises that not even Jamie Dimon, its apparently unseatable chairman and chief executive, can stay on top of. And that's to say nothing of the embarrassing example of the "London Whale," the nickname of Bruno Iksil, the JPMorgan trader who, in 2012, lost the company $6 billion through misguided internal "hedging." Given JPMorgan's size and the complexity of its operations, there is no good reason why it should not be split up.

Dodd-Frank and the Volcker Rule, its signature feature, were designed to force big banks to shrink their riskier businesses or get out of them altogether. But the five-year gap between rulemaking and implementation didn't inspire confidence. And though the rule finally went into effect in July 2015 (with some features delayed until 2017), its impact has been muted thus far—perhaps because, while they stalled for time, the big banks went ahead and restructured accordingly.

The question remains whether the rather cosmetic split between speculative trading and banking for customers has done much to reduce the big banks' status as "too big to fail." A number of articulate reformists say not. Elizabeth Warren, a Democratic senator, filed a bill in July 2015 calling for a new Glass-Steagall Act that would clearly separate the deposit-taking and trading activities of big banks. It would force big banks to choose between taking big risks with investors' money or being careful with depositors' money, but not mixing the two. If the Glass-Steagall Act of 1933 had been in place in 2008, says Dennis Kelleher of bank reform group Better Markets, "there's little doubt it would have lessened the depth and breadth of the crisis." Such is the power of the bank lobby, however, that unless a truly reforming president is elected in November 2016, Warren's bill is unlikely to become law.

A Note on Proprietary Trading Versus Market Making

What is the difference between proprietary trading (taking risk positions speculatively for the bank's own account), and market making (taking risk positions in anticipation of filling customer orders)?

In the United States, the Volcker Rule specifies that deposit-taking banks may not carry out proprietary trading, but that they may do market making. Similarly, the proposed German and French banking reform laws, and the European Commission's latest proposal on bank resilience, allow deposit-taking banks to do market making up to a certain threshold, but no proprietary trading.

The problem is how to make a distinction between the two. In both cases, banks take positions. Deciding what the intention was behind taking a particular position is no easier than playing poker. A glance at the complex criteria proposed by the five U.S. regulators for applying the Volcker Rule suggests it will not be easy to police. The rule depends on constant monitoring of trading desks by bankers and their regulators to ensure that market making—

> the business of being willing to facilitate customer purchases and sales of financial instru-

ments as an intermediary over time and in size,
including by holding positions in inventory

—has not become proprietary trading:

> the purchase or sale of one or more financial in-
> struments taken principally for the purpose of
> short-term resale, benefitting from short-term price
> movements, realizing short-term arbitrage profits,
> or hedging another trading account position.

The EU proposal for a regulation to improve the resilience
of credit institutions defines proprietary trading and market
making as follows:

> "Proprietary trading" means using own capital
> or borrowed money to take positions in any type
> of transaction to purchase, sell or otherwise ac-
> quire or dispose of any financial instrument or
> commodities for the sole purpose of making a
> profit for own account, and without any con-
> nection to actual or anticipated client activity
> or for the purpose of hedging the entity's risk
> as result of actual or anticipated client activity,
> through the use of desks, units, divisions or in-
> dividual traders specifically dedicated to such
> position taking and profit making, including
> through dedicated web-based proprietary trad-
> ing platforms.

> "Market making" means a financial institution's commitment to provide market liquidity on a regular and ongoing basis, by posting two-way quotes with regard to a certain financial instrument, or as part of its usual business, by fulfilling orders initiated by clients or in response to clients' requests to trade, but in both cases without being exposed to material market risk.

There is no better example of how well-intentioned regulators have got themselves, and the financial world, into a muddle by trying to accommodate existing practices, however opaque. A clear line in the sand would be better.

Germany: Does It Need a National Champion?

Are there lessons to be learned from Germany's banking structure?

Like its large British equivalents, Germany's Deutsche Bank is under threat of some kind of segmentation—thanks to Germany's bill on de-risking financial institutions. But otherwise, there are few cross-border similarities. It is most unlikely that Germany will break up its "national champion" completely. The Deutsche Bank group will continue to exist, most likely as nominally independent units under a holding company.

That said, Commerzbank, Deutsche's nearest private rival, continues to shrink into a more manageable, but less profitable, institution. Commerzbank is also an example of what can happen to a bank which sheds riskier businesses and a lot of investment bankers, and concentrates on its core customers. It becomes boring, less likely to make extraordinary profits, and a disappointment for its less enlightened shareholders. This presents a conundrum, but it's also progress—it's certainly preferable to the alternative arrangement, which helped get us into this mess in the first place. In my opinion, the answer to the conundrum is not to abandon reform. It is for the bank to find shareholders who have lower expectations. If that doesn't work, it should be taken over by the state, which, in the case of Commerzbank, still owns around 16 percent.

Germany's network of smaller banks (similar to that in Austria)—made up of savings banks (Sparkassen—which are municipally owned) and mutual banks (Volksbanken and Raiffeisenbanken)—could be a model for other countries to follow. These banks are of manageable size, have regional expertise, and have a simple business model. Their culture is not one of excessive rewards. The greatest danger they suffer from is local political interference—while the second greatest is being hoodwinked into bad investment decisions because of their lack of financial sophistication. Arguably, they may be too small and undiversified to serve the country's biggest companies (as proponents of the universal banking model assert), but they are able to procure services for them from bigger wholesale and commercial banks, such as the state-owned Landesbanken and the co-operative central bank, DZ Bank. It's true that both the Landesbanken and the DZ/WGZ Bank group ran into problems some time ago, because of a combination of political influence, delusions of grandeur, and bad risk management. But that doesn't disqualify the model itself. Now that some Landesbanken have disappeared through merger or closure, there are realistic hopes that the rest will be better managed, though the danger of political manipulation requires constant vigilance.

Germany's amended banking law, reflecting the European Union's Liikanen report, and harmonized with France's new law, envisages the transfer of a bank's trading and market-making activity, above a certain volume, to a separately capitalized entity. The aim is to ensure that if the trading entity fails there is no impact on the commercial bank and its insured customer deposits. The trading entity is free to take proprietary positions and to deal with hedge funds, while the commercial bank would lend to companies and to retail customers. However, there is an unresolved issue (just as there is with the Volcker Rule in the United States) about what constitutes market making and where that overlaps with, or runs over into, proprietary trading—in theory, market making is essentially neutral, but in practice, as we've seen, it's often not so simple.

Like the Liikanen proposal, the German law allows the trading and commercial-banking entities to be owned by the same holding company—provided there is no cross-funding or double counting of capital. This funding firewall has the same aim as the British ring-fencing concept, but bank lobbyists on both sides of the Channel continue to argue for some freedom to move free capital between the two entities. The European Council, which is still crafting an EU-wide version of regulation, gives national supervisors the discretion to allow universal banks, of which Deutsche Bank and BNP Paribas are classic examples, to continue to operate as a single firm, which threatens to make a nonsense of the entire ring-fencing exercise.

One quirk of the German law is the provision that managers who endanger the bank through reckless behavior can face criminal prosecution and a spell in jail. Legal experts have pointed out that there are huge difficulties with this. First, if the executive has behaved fraudulently—for instance, by allowing the bank to continue trading while insolvent, or by misleading shareholders in other ways—then prosecution for fraud would be simpler than prosecution under a banking law. Second, it would be extremely difficult to establish that a bad trading decision was "reckless" enough to endanger the bank, except through hindsight. The executive could contend that, given the information he or she had at the time, it was a reasonable decision. The danger is that every trading decision that goes bad might become the subject of a lawsuit.

An analysis of the last banking crisis suggests that many bankers may have traded recklessly and endangered their institutions. But, to a large extent, they were encouraged to do so by failures of supervision and regulation. They made over-optimistic assumptions about liquidity and the buoyancy of the market—but so did their regulators. Both bankers and regulators should have learned something from this lesson. So if bad bankers deserve to be jailed in future, so do bad regulators.

Beyond Liikanen

At the end of January 2014, the European Commission published a proposal for a regulation, based on consultations after the Liikanen report, to "improve the resilience of EU credit institutions." The nub of it is a ban on proprietary trading in credit institutions above a certain size. Any such trading would have to be done in a legally and economically separate entity. But a year later, the proposal had been considerably watered down by the European Parliament's Monetary Affairs Committee, and by June 2015, an even weaker version was put out by the European Council. The Council basically referred the decision on how, or even whether, proprietary trading should be separated from banking back to national authorities. It fought shy of imposing any kind of structure, such as a holding company framework, on existing banking groups.

The proposal in its present shape attempts to harmonize some of the national legislation already in train. But in doing so it looks as though it will allow the universal banking model to survive almost intact—provided the competent authority can put up a decent argument. Any structural reforms under EU auspices are not expected to be enforced until 2018 or 2019, though individual countries may get there earlier. The French law required the transfer of proprietary trading to a separate entity by the beginning of 2015, German law by the beginning of 2016, but there is no evidence that this has happened yet. National authorities are reluctant to put their banks at a disadvantage.

The Euro Zone and the Forfeiture of Sovereignty

Inevitably, European banks that fall under CRD 4 and other pending EU legislation have their own peculiar systemic problems. Two stand out:

1. The proposed Banking Union, which means that banks within the euro zone will, ultimately, no longer be creatures of their home government.
2. CRD 4, which, at the standardized level applied to all but the most sophisticated banks, counts home-government bonds on bank balance sheets as zero-risk weighted. Naturally, this stretches credibility to the limit as far as Greek and Portuguese banks—and even Spanish and Italian banks—and their holdings of national government bonds are concerned.

In my opinion, this is the point at which the euro-zone crisis—and all the anomalies that it has thrown up—has a direct bearing on global bank reform. If euro-zone government debt ever became "mutual" (i.e., jointly and severally guaranteed) it might be possible to sustain the convention applied outside the euro-zone: that government debt of a bank's domicile, in its home currency, is zero-risk weighted.

But if there continues to be wide divergence in euro-zone sovereign ratings, then bonds issued by individual euro-zone countries must, at some point, cease to qualify as risk-free assets for their home banks. That will continue to put euro-zone banks at a disadvantage compared with banks of "normal" countries, whose governments have sovereign control of monetary policy. (Although periodic jitters over U.S. T-bills during recent budget crises, in 2013 and 2015, suggest that there are doubts about the risk-free quality of even U.S. Treasury debt.)

As I see it there are four possible outcomes:

1. Euro-zone regulators will continue to regard these bonds as risk-free—which is what current EU bank regulation does.
2. They will apply a "haircut" to liquidity reserves that include government bonds that trade at a discount.
3. They will require banks in countries whose government bonds trade at a discount to replace them with more highly rated bonds in their liquidity reserve.
4. Euro-zone banks will opt for another kind of liquidity buffer, built from another kind of asset. Central bank money has been suggested.

Assuming euro-zone regulators continue with the Banking Union plan, the biggest banks, under the supervision of the European Central Bank, will be governed by a single bank resolution mechanism, a common resolution fund, and, ultimately, common deposit insurance.

But there are other legislative troubles in the EU. Take the financial transaction tax (FTT), which was supposed to be implemented by eleven of the twenty-eight countries at the beginning of 2016, but is now on hold until the next deadline—June 2016. (And that's the best-case scenario.) Only Italy has unilaterally imposed a tax. A Europe-wide FTT was threatened by a legal challenge on the grounds that it should not be applied by stealth in the seventeen EU countries that do not support the idea. Although that argument failed, British chancellor George Osborne remains opposed, and at the end of 2015, Estonia—originally one of the countries willing to introduce the tax—opted out. That the parameters of the tax are modest has done nothing to dissuade the opposition.

In an attempt to change bank culture, and reduce the incentive for bank employees to bet the bank, the EU also imposed a cap on bonuses from the beginning of 2014, at a maximum of 200 percent of base salary. Predictably those banks renowned for paying high bonuses found ways around the speed limit. Deutsche Bank gave its staff a "fixed pay adjustment" at the end of 2014, as well as showering 1,100 of its top talent with an extra $300 million in "additional fixed pay supplements." Barclays invented a concept called "role-based pay" allowing it to double the base salary of employees who boasted particular "seniority, depth and breadth." The British Bankers Association still complains that the bonus cap puts EU banks at a "structural disadvantage" when competing outside EU territory.

Switzerland

What about the beleaguered Swiss? FINMA, the Swiss financial watchdog, has attempted to rein in its two big systemically relevant banks, UBS and Credit Suisse, by demanding extra capital and liquidity under the Swiss parliament's "too big to fail" legislation. In response, the two banks have gone down very different routes: UBS has severely reduced its investment-banking coverage and is concentrating on wealth management, while Credit Suisse is still competing with other global investment banks in global markets. UBS has nearly three times as many employees involved in wealth management as Credit Suisse. Credit Suisse is carrying 30 percent more risk-weighted assets in its investment banking and global markets than UBS. Yet their leverage ratios (according to stringent Swiss criteria) were equal at 3.9 percent at the end of September 2015. Not satisfied with this, the Swiss government raised the bar even higher in October 2015, increasing the leverage ratio to 5 percent, to be phased in, with other bank-strengthening measures, by 2019. Since a failure of one of these banks would devastate the country's economy, the drive to end their "too big to fail" status goes on. But not even the Swiss regulator has got to grips with the real problem with these institutions: like their foreign rivals, they are hostage to a rotten incentive culture.

Part Two

REVOLUTION

3

THE NEED FOR A NEW MODEL

The evidence that I've laid out in Part 1 of this book has led me to a single, clear conclusion: we need a new model of banking (and to an extent a reworking of the entire financial system), so that it is less likely to need rescue by the taxpayer and is more likely to serve the real economy, not a narrow interest group.

It is understandable that, in the present economic climate, governments are reluctant to do more than tinker with the system for fear of incurring further costs—and the further wrath of the taxpayer.

But this is a blinkered, short-term view. We owe it to future generations to get it right, or more right, this time. This wouldn't be unprecedented: after all, if Glass-Steagall had been kept in place, it can be argued that the world would not have gotten into such a mess over the last decade. This is the grand scale on which we need to be thinking.

Can we design a banking and financial system that won't in turn be unpicked by future generations? I think we can.

But I also think it requires a major intellectual leap in how we think about banking.

Utility Principle

First of all, perhaps we should think of the financial system as a utility, in the same way that we think of sewage systems and elec-

tricity distribution. After all, the basic functions of finance are to facilitate payments and keep track of cash balances. Banks must also
safeguard deposits, pay them back on demand or on maturity, and
make credit judgments on borrowers. All of this is very important,
but it isn't especially glamorous.

To inspire confidence, banks have tended to be housed in
prestigious buildings. That has come to obfuscate their basic
function and has given bankers an exaggerated sense of their
own importance. Victorian sewage works and pumping stations
were also housed in prestigious buildings, but there was no illu-
sion about the stuff they were pumping. When it comes to banks,
there is. Part of the confusion that has arisen (both in bankers'
sense of their own importance and in the eyes of the broader society) comes from the contrast between the basic functions of banking and the considerable power that some bankers have wielded
in the past, from financing wars to bailing out countries. But the
recent financial crisis has shown, more strongly than previous
crises, that banking activity can readily impose a cost on society—and that this cost is not taken into account when rewards
are distributed among banks' investors and employees.

Let's try to break down what exactly banks and bankers *do*.

Basic Retail Banking

The building blocks of a financial system, commonly understood,
are banks, a central bank, and a set of rules that govern how they
should operate. Key to that is the retail bank.

First and foremost, ordinary men and women (who can

also be seen as voters and taxpayers) need a reliable place to keep their cash. A bank is generally more reliable than the underside of a mattress. To maintain confidence in that bank, it must be governed by soundness principles and conduct-of-business rules. Experience also shows that retail deposits are "stickiest"—most stable and long-lasting—if there is some kind of deposit insurance, either from the government or from a deposit-insurance fund, or preferably both. Further soundness is secured if limits are set on how those bank deposits are used.

Even though there are always limits on what a bank can do with your money, that point is worth pressing further. For instance, a "narrow bank" (to use the economist John Kay's term), the soundest bank thinkable, would be allowed to invest only in domestic government bonds of short-term maturity. Deposits at a "narrow bank" could conceivably have an explicit 100 percent government guarantee. Such a bank would indeed be sound— but it might be *too* sound.* Rather than gaining a meager return on government bonds, a proportion of the deposits might

---

* A few respected economists argue that a banking union across the euro zone can best be reached by reintroducing the notion of retail deposits that are 100 percent insured with reserves at the central bank—i.e., backed by risk-free central bank money. It is only in this way, they say, that deposit insurance will work regardless of which country the bank is registered in. Effectively, it would eliminate political influence on bank behavior.

This might make sense—provided that the 100 percent reserves cover only the insured deposits. Other bank deposits, which would not be backed in this way, would pay a competitive rate of interest—and would be used to finance lending and the economy in general. Depositors would be aware that these deposits are at risk, but would be rewarded with higher interest rates.

prudently be put to work. Experience has shown that banks can reasonably extend their investments to (modest) mortgage lending and personal and small-company loans—at least, up to a strictly limited proportion of deposits.

In all cases, any bank, no matter how narrow, would need a level of capital to tide it over periods where late payment or losses on loans exceed the net inflow of deposits and loan service payments.

In the end, retail banks must be so robust that their failure is near-impossible. Deposit insurance—implicitly or explicitly backed by the government—means that a run on a retail bank is unlikely, unless the government itself faces bankruptcy. (We've seen this scenario play out all too vividly over the last two years, but that's not a banking problem—it's a problem of state solvency.) Because even conservatively managed retail banks tend to be allowed to make home loans and to take liens on property as security on small-business loans, they are inevitably exposed to housing and commercial property busts. But, in the eyes of the broader society, that is generally considered an acceptable and manageable risk, provided regulators insist on low loan-to-value ratios.

To be absolutely clear: *retail banks are not meant to be completely bombproof.* A simple retail bank does not need to be bombproof if it is a financial institution that the government cares about and would support in a crisis. But this would be the only kind of bank that would have such implicit or explicit support. Wiseacres will say it was retail banks, such as HBOS and Northern Rock, that got into most trouble during the crisis. The fact is, these were not simple retail banks; they were heavily interconnected with other financial players, and they had contingent lines of credit to supposedly remote strategic investment vehicles (SIVs) that they had to honor in the face of a liquidity crisis. Regulators should never have allowed them to extend themselves in that way. In April 2007, the UK's Financial Services Authority actually advised Northern Rock that it was under-using its capital and could afford to expand its business. In the United States, Washington Mutual, which was taken over by JPMorgan Chase as crisis struck in September 2008, was an example of a retail and mortgage bank which expanded beyond its retail brief, including buying wholesale mortgage loans, exposing itself to starvation of short-term funding. Likewise, Countrywide Financial, on the face of it a simple mortgage bank, was heavily exposed to the most toxic parts of mortgage securitizations at the time of its rescue by Bank of America in January 2008. Those banks found plenty of willing creditors and investors in the wild days before the crisis.

But who would invest in a truly safe, boring retail bank today? A deposit-taking bank that makes a modest amount of mortgage and retail loans, and invests the balance in government bonds, is unlikely to make a heady return on investment. So it would attract only the most conservative investors. A return on equity of more than 6 percent is unlikely. The government might even have to subsidize the business to make it attract any investors at all. But it would be safe. On balance, that would be in the long-term interest of customers and taxpayers.

If the financial system can be thought of as a utility, one could certainly view this kind of retail banking as a key facet thereof—part of the necessary infrastructure of a properly functioning society. This, would not rule out state or municipal ownership, though in that case, the trick would be to keep banks out of the hands of hungry politicians. As we've seen, the experience of the German Sparkassen is that they can be very useful for supporting local businesses. But they are also in danger of being steered toward supporting prestige projects and other vote-catching schemes by local politicians and other board members. That's a big problem—but it is not insuperable.

Corporate and Wholesale Banking

Bigger companies also need a bank that can handle complex cash flows, provide them with foreign-exchange and other services, pre-finance projects, offer buyer credits to their customers, and support them through mergers, disposals, and acquisitions. They also need advisers to take them through the issuing of new shares or bonds, and perhaps to provide commodity hedges and other derivatives.

The question is: Are these services best provided by a one-stop commercial-cum-investment bank? Or should there be a clear distinction between commercial/wholesale banking and what we know as investment banking?

And, whatever the answer to that, are there dangers in allowing a single bank to provide such services? For instance, are there unmanageable conflicts of interest? And is a bank that sees all these flows likely to front-run its clients?

In my opinion, a sensible division of labor would be for the commercial/wholesale bank to provide customers with lending, cash management, and standard foreign-exchange and interest-rate hedging services, but to outsource anything more complex to an investment bank. It could also provide financial support to investment banks—but only to a limited extent, and with appropriate credit and performance-risk controls so that the interconnectedness that made the collapse of Lehman Brothers so traumatic is avoided. Commercial/wholesale banks should not be allowed to make their balance sheets available for investment banks, or other shadow banks, as a place to "park" underwriting positions and other trading exposures.

A commercial/wholesale bank would need to be a critical size to achieve economies of scale. But those economies of scale must not involve cross-subsidy from a retail operation.* Nor should the commercial/wholesale bank be integrated with an investment bank to produce a bank so large and powerful that, along with other similar beasts, it could control pricing in the market.

Universal banks, such as JPMorgan Chase, Barclays, and Deutsche Bank not only provide these one-stop-shop services to corporate clients. They also take retail deposits, and they have

---

* There is always an exception. Many have pointed to Sweden's Handelsbanken as a model retail bank that also deals with corporate customers. Handelsbanken is well worth a study as an example of a bank that has limited itself to the clients and businesses that it understands, and which has a bonus system which pays out only at retirement and treats chief executive and doorman as equals (apart, reportedly, from a handful of vital investment bankers). Cross-subsidy from the retail operation does not appear to be an issue while its corporate bank is so conservative and profitable. The Handelsbanken model is impressive, but it is very selective, so could probably not be replicated nationwide to provide inclusive retail and corporate banking.

clients on the investment side that buy the securities that they issue for corporations. The retail deposits offer these universal banks a stability, and access to cheap money, that they would not otherwise enjoy. But for the retail depositor there is no obvious benefit in putting his deposits at risk with a bank that lends to big companies and deals in world markets. The depositor has no chance of sharing in the upside if the bank makes egregious profits. But he, or the taxpayer/deposit insurer, has a risk that the bank makes egregious losses. No one testifying to the Vickers Commission or the Liikanen group of high-level experts was able to volunteer a good reason why retail customers might benefit from putting deposits with a corporate and investment bank. It is only universal bankers themselves who talk of the stability that these deposits offer the bank (because they cross-subsidize other parts of their business).

Of course, it is inevitable that corporate/wholesale banks that are not cross-subsidized by retail deposits will be more costly to run. Corporate financial services may therefore be more expensive. But that will reflect the real cost of doing business. If governments decide that they need to subsidize the development of certain business sectors, they can do that with loan schemes, tax breaks, or even via development funds, or perhaps a development bank—all of which would be more transparent than the current system of hidden subsidies.

It is also inevitable that there will be a distinction between financial services provided to less sophisticated fund managers or private investors, and those provided to investors qualified as professional counterparties. In a simple division of labour, corporate/wholesale banks would provide basic financial services—such as cash management, custody, and foreign exchange—direct to investment clients. They would outsource more sophisticated services—such as the buying and selling of securities, derivatives, and other hedging instruments—to brokers or investment banks, acting as agent only—provided the client is sufficiently sophisticated and its articles of association allow it to use such instruments.

Sophisticated investors might thus use corporate/wholesale banks as custodians and to provide simple financial services, but for more sophisticated trades they would need to use a broker, or an investment bank.

"Pure" Merchant and Investment Banking

A partnership is generally reckoned to be the best model for a merchant or investment bank. In it, the partners put their own capital at risk. That makes sense. An investment bank provides advice and transaction services to clients, underwriting—if only briefly—the placing of shares or bonds, and taking equity or lending stakes to launch new ventures or reshape existing ones. The partners share unlimited personal liability for net losses sustained by the partnership.

I advocate a return of investment banking to the partnership model.

This is not simply to put the clock back to an alleged "golden age" of investment banking; it is because there is a better alignment of interests between partners and the bank. Partners are also less likely to give employees incentives to trade recklessly, given their interest in the fortunes, good or bad, of the bank of which they are owners.*

Whose Capital?

Equity investors in private listed companies expect a return, either through a dividend or through capital growth. When that company is heavily regulated—as in the case of a water utility or a bank—investor expectations are slightly different. Heavy regulation normally means the company is likely to have steadier, but lower, profits.

Recently, investors in banks have sought consistently high returns—but have instead got more volatile returns, anything from 25 percent to a negative return on equity (ROE). A more stable financial sector would attract the utility-type investor, but not the chaser of high risk/high return. Can a reformed and stable financial sector offer investors attractive enough returns? Probably not, unless investors sharply lower their expectations.

Recent share issues by banks such as Deutsche Bank and Barclays have suggested a cost of capital for major international banks of around 10 percent. This means that a Deutsche Bank, Barclays, Credit Suisse, or BNP Paribas would have to aim for a

---

* Supporters of the universal banking model will say that only universal banks—one-stop shops—can offer full banking services to the world's biggest corporations. But there is a counterargument: these big corporations already buy services from more than one financial institution. For the really big deals they usually hire a consortium of banks and/or investment banks. They do not, and should not, use banks as one-stop shops.

return on equity of 15 percent or more: these days, they are lucky if they produce a 5 percent return.

Given the heavy regulatory and compliance burdens that are placed on institutions categorized as systemically important, it is a huge challenge for banks to produce an ROE consistently over 10 percent. The risk (and it is a risk grounded in the recklessness that preceded the financial crisis) is that the bank's executives will "massage" returns rather than concentrate on the bank's stability and on improving service to customers. Some adjustment of investors' expectations is therefore necessary. But it is worth emphasizing that investors might also benefit from two positive effects. Simplifying banks (and banking rules) would

- reduce operating costs and the cost of compliance and regulation;
- and, in the longer run, reduce the cost of financial services to both borrowers and investors.

4

HOW TO GET THERE FROM HERE: 10 REMEDIES

This is the tricky bit . . .

Even those who concede that the current system is in many ways dysfunctional are inclined to give up. We are where we are, and it would be utopian to believe in radical change. Maybe, maybe not. Certainly, the direction of banking reform since the 2008 crisis has not inspired confidence. It is not leading to the new banking world outlined above; nor has it offered coherent answers to the shortcomings that were outlined in part 1.

As I see it, the two most glaring failures are:

- the failure to simplify the complexity; and
- the failure to change the culture that permeates the world of finance.

The big banks that dominate world finance today are still too big and too complex. Proposals to break them into smaller, more manageable pieces have been resisted tooth and nail by politicians and bankers alike—and even by regulators, either because of "capture" or because they, too, are scared of radical change. The culture of entitlement by bankers to a disproportionate share of the financial spoils persists at regulated banks, even at those owned by thousands of small shareholders, or even by the state.

A new and tougher approach is needed. Big banks must be broken up—and that means not just into "good" banks and "bad" banks. Functions that lead inevitably to conflicts of interest and to client abuse must be separated. Opaque cross-subsidy must end. So must oligopolistic behavior by institutions and groups of people within institutions.

So: how to do it?

1. Simplify the Rules . . .

Most social activities need rules. Rulemakers usually strive to keep them to a minimum to keep things simple for participants and enforcers. But regulation of financial services has, in recent years, been a race to complexity: the more complex the services offered, the more regulators have attempted to capture that complexity in their rules.

This must stop. It is time to go back to first principles and ask: What are the simplest rules that financial markets and institutions need in order to function? If certain financial instruments and practices don't fit inside the simplified rulebook because they are too complex to describe, then they should be exiled to the part of the market that is "unregulated."* (It should cheer the regulation-phobic that, in my new world, the territory occupied

---

* This is already happening to some extent, since banks have been encouraged (by Basel III rules) to clear standard over-the-counter (OTC) derivatives contracts on exchanges. According to market reports, hedge funds and other "shadow banks" are taking some of this business from the big banks active in derivatives.

by investment banks, hedge funds and the like will be less hamstrung by rules than before, on the principle of caveat emptor.)

2. Scrap Basel II and III . . .

The Basel Committee on Banking Supervision took a wrong turning in the 1990s, and began to collude with the way that bankers themselves want to run their banks. Sound banking must be brought back to first principles. Rule No. 1 is that *risk models used by banks for their own trading advantage should not also function as supervisory tools.* That, unfortunately, means that the foundation on which Basel II and Basel III are based, allowing the use of approved internal models by so-called "sophisticated" banks to set their own capital charges, must be scrapped. True, it also means that risk measures will be cruder, but they will be standardized and applied to all banks. Provided the banks meet those crude standard measures, such as a leverage ratio and broad-brush common risk weightings, they can still use their internal models for trading advantage.

3. "De-Game" Risk Weights . . .

The concept of risk-weighted assets (RWAs) is superficially beguiling. Some assets are surely more risky than others. If regulatory capital ratios are too crude, then there is a danger that banks will "game" them and put riskier assets in loopholes not caught by these ratios. This is indeed a risk—one that needs to be monitored by supervisors and all stakeholders in the bank. *But the principle of allowing banks to calculate their own risk weightings for regulatory purposes must go.*

4. Put a Cap on Absolute Size . . .

It is probably true that absolute size alone does not determine how manageable a bank is. On the other hand, a landscape of giant banks makes management extraordinarily difficult. Moreover, it tends to stifle competition and to tilt the balance between practitioners, regulators, and politicians. And, of course, as we've seen, it is not clear that economies of scale get better for banks with assets beyond $100 billion.

In my opinion, *splitting existing global banks into three stand-alone entities* (retail; corporate/wholesale; investment banking) will go some way to reduce each unit's balance sheet, and increase its manageability, but more reduction may be needed.

5. Reduce Interconnectedness . . .

We mustn't give up on this. There are ways to limit interconnectedness between banks, and between banks and nonbanks. We need to use them.

The interbank lending market has already shrunk since 2007 because of more sensitivity about banks' and national banking sectors' creditworthiness, and more recently because of the scandal involving manipulation of Libor, the most common interbank lending benchmark. A financial transaction tax, which makes repo transactions (the lending or sale and buyback of securities) more expensive, would further reduce interconnectedness. But ending regulated banks' exposure as prime brokers and lenders of leveraged loans to hedge funds and private-equity firms is the key. Flatly outlawing such exposure is the best remedy. The risk arising from interconnectedness would then be confined to the community of investment banks, hedge funds, private-equity firms, and sophisticated investors that deal with each other.

6. Put the Credit Derivatives Toothpaste Back in the Tube . . .

Given the damage wrought over the past twenty years by the misunderstanding and misuse of credit derivatives, a rethink is necessary.

One big problem with credit derivatives is that they offer banks and investors a means of getting credit exposure without having to study or research the underlying credit risk. Since one of a bank's core functions is the handling of credit, this is a lazy way of taking exposure—or of protecting the balance sheet. It takes us away from a world in which banks have firsthand experience of the companies and other borrowers they do business with. Attempts have been made to restrict the purchase of credit default swaps (CDS) to those who have exposure to the underlying credit risk. It might be difficult for regulators to prevent the bilateral writing of CDSs, but regulated banks and insurance companies could conceivably be forbidden to write them and/or trade them.

7. Encourage New Banks . . .

Creation of new banks in all three categories (retail, wholesale/ commercial, and investment/shadow) should be encouraged, and barriers to entry lowered across the board. In the retail sector, this would mean encouragement of anything from "narrow" banks to mutual banks, co-operative banks, communal savings banks, credit unions, standard high-street or small-town banks, and person-to-person lending operations such as Zopa and Lending Club. Most retail banks tend to rely on a credit bureau to help them decide on credit terms for each borrower. As these credit bureau scores proliferate, person-to-person lending and lending by credit unions may grow more commonplace, offering more competition to incumbent retail banks.

In particular, I would like to see more wholesale/commercial banks. This would be a new class of bank for the Anglo-Saxon world: it would have no retail deposit base, yet it would make both corporate and wholesale loans. Its business model would be similar to that of a German Landesbank, but without the Landesbank's historical flaws.* It would fund itself in the securities markets and by taking deposits from corporate and retail banks, though not from retail customers.

---

* Most German Landesbanken, even those that survived the recent crisis, have a bad reputation after years of poor risk management and delusions of grandeur. One exception might be Hessische Landesbank (though that may be because of its robust risk-management pact, Verbund, with regional savings banks). But there is no obvious reason why a corporate/wholesale bank should be as badly run as the Landesbanken were. It would be designed to serve its client base, not to pile extra risks on its balance sheet because of over-cheap funding.

The work of these banks could possibly be complemented and supported (for instance, with partial guarantees) by a development bank along the lines of Germany's state-owned Kreditanstalt für Wiederaufbau (KfW). The closest equivalent of such a model in the United States may be the "wholesale bank," as defined by the Community Reinvestment Act. These banks have to meet certain criteria, including having a role in community development, to be recognized by regulators such as the Federal Deposit Insurance Corporation. These wholesale banks do not take retail deposits or make retail loans, though they deal with banks that do. A British equivalent, but on a small scale, is the British Business Bank, which was set up by the government in 2014 to support small and medium-size firms.

It should be possible to keep the operation of corporate/wholesale banks quite simple. Their core function is to finance companies, municipalities, governments (and perhaps other banks), to offer them a range of other financial services such as foreign-exchange and interest-rate products, and to facilitate such things as bond and share issues. As commercial banks, not investment banks, they would not lead-manage such issues, but they might underwrite part of a bond or share issue for a short time. It is not their business to trade in and out of bonds, shares, derivatives, or other financial instruments for their own account, or even to make markets for clients.

The closest the commercial/wholesale banks might get to conventional investment banking would be lead-managing the financing of a giant project, such as a nuclear power station. There, they would spread the credit risk with other corporate/wholesale banks or engage the services of an investment bank to find nonbank lenders such as investment funds or infrastructure funds. Each bank would be limited to lending only a portion of its overall capital to a single borrower, or to a business sector, such as commercial property, shipping, the automotive industry, etc.

8. Leave the Shadow Banks Alone . . .

While parts of the financial industry will see more constraint and regulation, others will see very little: investment banking partnerships will have the freedom to work closely with the rest of the shadow-banking sector, in which I include hedge funds, private-equity firms, and other alternative investment managers. The only restriction on their activity will be that their financing must not come from regulated retail or corporate/wholesale banks. Instead, they will need to finance themselves by the issue of bonds and commercial paper (of which corporate/wholesale banks may hold only a limited amount), and by tapping hedge funds and other investment funds directly for private placements of debt, equity, or subordinated debt and project-specific investments.

Regulators will need to look only at the aggregate numbers, for macro-prudential—big-picture—reasons. If, for example, the commercial property market seemed in danger of overheating, regulators might caution the corporate/wholesale banks and discourage their further lending to the sector. But they would not directly intervene in the activities of the alternative investors.

In my new world, anyone would be able to start his or her own investment bank—just as anyone can start his or her own hedge fund. The aim would be to keep this sector as unregulated as possible. However, as a counterparty/clearing member of a stock exchange or other exchange, an investment bank would still have to meet the capital and liquidity requirements set by the exchange, as well as its "fit and proper person" requirements. In the United States, dealers in securities and the firms themselves would have to satisfy the criteria of FINRA, the nongovernment Financial Industry Regulatory Authority. Otherwise, the investment bank's ability to use leverage will depend only on its relationship with its sources of funding (which will not be regulated banks).

9. Offer a Light Touch to Hedge Funds, Pension Funds, and Other Institutional Investors . . .

There should be no need to regulate hedge funds or their managers for anything other than fraud, provided (a) that they are not dealing with vulnerable clients, such as financially illiterate or unsophisticated investors; and (b) that they are not getting finance or borrowing securities from a regulated retail or corporate/wholesale bank, or from a regulated pension or insurance fund.

In my new banking world, regulated pension or insurance funds would not be able to invest directly more than a small proportion (say 5 percent to 10 percent of their assets) in funds run by hedge fund managers or unregulated shadow banks. In other words, hedge funds, private equity funds, and other shadow banks (and the new-style investment banks) would be starved of the kind of cheap leverage they had in the past. They would then need to draw their capital and leverage either from each other, or from sophisticated private investors. The investment sector is likely to divide itself into two classes: those vehicles that have dealings with regulated entities and those that do not.

10. At Least Consider a Financial Transactions Tax . . .

It is no surprise that financial actors in general and the City of London in particular are against the imposition of an EU-wide financial transactions tax. The basic idea behind an FTT is to "throw sand in the wheels of capitalism"—although it has also been promoted as a "Robin Hood" tax to take some of the turn made by wheeler-dealers and distribute it among the less well-off. Inevitably, therefore, it is an emotional subject.

In my opinion, however, the *principle* of discouraging apparently "empty" trading (i.e., those trades between financial intermediaries with no end user in sight, which produce little in the way of concrete economic value, and which are often canceled before execution anyway) is not a bad one.

Would an FTT do *real* damage? I am skeptical. Some experts have objected that it would kill the market for repurchase agreements (repos) and security lending—cheap ways for owners of securities to raise short-term finance, or for market bears to short stocks. Since there are about $18 trillion of repos outstanding at any one time in the American and European markets (according to rough calculations by the New York Fed and the International Capital Market Association [ICMA]), this would seem to be a big deal. The planned EU tax will charge each repo trade at 0.1 percent regardless of maturity, so it will tend to inhibit the shorter-term contracts—the type heavily used by hedge funds and shadow banks. "The shrivelling of the repo market and the lack of viable alternatives would pose serious problems to institutional and corporate investors," claimed an analysis by ICMA in 2013. But there are concerns anyway among regulators about the sheer size of this untransparent market, and its increasing use by banks to window-dress their assets. If the FTT has a dampening effect on this practice, and on high-frequency trading, there is no obvious reason why end investors would suffer.

5

THE CHANGING FACE OF BANKING CAREERS

The biggest challenge facing employees (and their bosses) in the banking sector that I envisage is how they and their successors will live with much lower expectations: lower pay, less excitement, and, most important, less chance of hitting the jackpot and never having to work again.

Some may choose to move to the pure investment banking and alternative investment sector. But there they will have to live with risk of losses as well as gains. In my opinion, that will be healthier. Many who worked in finance in heady times during the past two decades knew they were being overpaid—but could hardly refuse the money thrown at them. Others may genuinely have believed they were adding value. But most of the value was going to them and their own institution, rather than to the clients they were supposed to be serving.

In the brave new world of sensible financial regulation that I am advocating, *this will change*. Instead, there will be more room for people who genuinely want to serve the real economy. There will also be more room for honest entrepreneurs who are willing (indeed, keen) to operate in an environment that puts them at risk of loss as well as gain.

6

SORTING OUT THE UNITED STATES

There is much work to do on the structure and culture of U.S. banking. Eight years since the crisis, the biggest U.S. banks are back doing business as usual. Even the Volcker Rule, designed to push proprietary trading into nonbank entities, has not truly hurt their ability to dominate trading markets around the world. Attempts at curbing the bonus culture were thwarted back in 2009.

Celebrated banker Jamie Dimon continues as both chairman and chief executive of JPMorgan Chase, apparently supported by regulators and shareholders, despite the $6 billion loss by the London Whale, and despite numerous cases where conflicts of interest were shown to be mishandled. And bank shareholders do not seem overly bothered by fines and settlements that directly damaged shareholder returns.

Bank of America, Citigroup, and JPMorgan have been fined in the past few years for manipulation of foreign-exchange markets; JPMorgan has been fined for failure to disclose conflicts of interest. These three banks, and also Goldman Sachs and Morgan Stanley, made multimillion-dollar settlements with the Securities & Exchange Commission following charges of misleading clients on complex securities transactions. These punishments may have checked some specific bad behavior for a while, but they have signally failed to affect governance or modify the incentive culture. Both need urgent attention.

Only a few voices are pressing for more radical reform, among them four senators led by Elizabeth Warren. Their new Glass-Steagall Act would go further than the watered-down Volcker Rule and prohibit banks with insured deposits from any affiliation with insurance, securities, or swaps entities, and from investing in complex financial products. No director or employee could serve simultaneously at an insured deposit taker and a securities or insurance firm, except at the discretion of the regulator. That might be enough to split up JPMorgan Chase and force Goldman Sachs out of the deposit-taking business. But it would not match the original Glass-Steagall Act, which split brokers and banks forever (or at least for sixty years) into separate companies. I would go further and devise a law that splits a leviathan such as JPMorgan into three differently named and unaffiliated entities: a lightly regulated investment-banking partnership, a wholesale corporate bank, and a retail bank that takes insured deposits (as outlined in Chapter 3).

Warren's bill is a breath of fresh air, yet it comes eight years after the event. Another voice for reform is Better Markets, a Washington-based lobby group, which has battled since 2010 against Wall Street's unerring ability to buy political influence and the big banks' resistance to change. Led by Dennis Kelleher, a lawyer and former Senate advisor, it regularly opines on financial rulemaking. But who is listening to their calls for change? And what can be done to change the culture at the biggest U.S. banks?

A good start, if lawmakers had the guts to do it, is to severely limit the level of employee remuneration at banks that take insured deposits, to an absolute cap of, say, $500,000. These banks are subsidized by the taxpayer, so there should legitimately be some official control over levels of pay.

Shareholders and enforcers should take more seriously the dodgy dealings uncovered between big banks and industry, politics, and even the criminal world. Look no further than a prolonged campaign led by Helen Davis Chaitman and Lance Gotthoffer, two New York lawyers, to expose links between JPMorgan Chase and Bernie Madoff, a convicted Ponzi schemer (see www.jpmadoff.com). There's also the matter of a case filed against JPMorgan for mishandling the funds of Christ Church Cathedral in Indianapolis: the investments were allegedly stuffed, contrary to all instructions, into high-risk rather than low-risk assets.

Such public exposure does not seem to be pushing officialdom or shareholders into holding a bank's top officers to account. Nor do the bankers themselves seem to relate the high level of their rewards to basic corporate or client responsibility. A revolt by shareholders would be the most effective way of forcing change. But that is not going to happen. Hence the need for far more radical steps by lawmakers and enforcers, even now, so long after the start of the crisis.

7

SORTING OUT BRITAIN

In any rethink about the future of the financial system and the financial sector, *Britain is a special case*—not least because the financial sector has come to dominate the British economy and to crowd out other (arguably more useful) economic activity.

I acknowledge that several attempts have been made since 2008 to change the nature of Britain's big incumbent banks and the prevailing culture. These attempts have signally failed. In particular, UK Financial Investments (UKFI), which, as the major shareholder, had the opportunity to make its mark on RBS and Lloyds Banking Group, failed to precipitate change in either the structure of these banks or their management culture. In my opinion, stronger medicine is needed.

What should that medicine include? It seems to me that there are three steps to be taken:

1. Nationalization

In my opinion, RBS and (possibly) Lloyds Banking Group, two of Britain's four biggest banks, should be fully nationalized. This may seem a drastic step, and it is. But it is the only lever the government has to send a clear message that the prevailing culture must change.*

In the five years since the rescue of RBS and Lloyds, successive UK governments have failed to make a dent in the way these banks are run or in the way that rewards are shared out. More radical measures are necessary—perhaps with existing private shareholders being offered nonvoting preference shares in an equity-for-debt swap. Other "limping" institutions, such as Nationwide and the Co-op Bank, might also be nationalized. This would give the government a free hand to appoint the management it wants, and to determine remuneration practices throughout these institutions.

Who would run these nationalized banks? They would certainly have to be exceptional people, prepared to take home a fraction of their predecessors' pay, yet able to preside over the conversion of a behemoth into smaller autonomous units. They might be seconded from accounting or consulting firms—but only on the understanding that they would be paid by the bank, not the seconding firm. I am confident such people exist—and that they would come forward.

True, the EU's Competition Commissioner might object that nationalization amounts to state aid and demand that the banks be returned to the private sector as soon as possible. (However, the Directorate-General for Competition says it is agnostic on whether a concern is privately or state-owned, provided the

---

* I have an unlikely ally in Nigel Lawson, former Chancellor of the Exchequer (1983–88), who wrote of RBS in a *Financial Times* article in November 2013: "The government blundered by acquiring only 81 per cent, rather than 100 per cent, of the equity. The existence of the minority shareholding continues to complicate the process of sorting out the RBS mess in the public interest."

state is not propping it up commercially.) Moreover, Britain could point to many examples of state ownership in other EU countries to which the EU turns a blind eye.

2. Breaking Up the Big Banks

For Britain's four or five biggest banks, I believe that there must be a clear split of investment banking from commercial banking (not just a separation of proprietary trading and prime brokerage for hedge funds, as recommended by Liikanen), and a ring-fencing of retail banking from both commercial and investment banking (as recommended by Vickers). The cleanest solution, in my opinion, would be a separation of each big bank—RBS, Lloyds, HSBC, and Barclays (and perhaps Standard Chartered and Santander)—into three stand-alone entities: retail, commercial/wholesale, and investment banks.

Obviously, the retail and commercial/wholesale banks must be very strongly capitalized. Only then can any "spare" capital be assigned to the investment bank. But that is not enough. As soon as possible, the ownership of the investment bank must be restructured into a partnership—via a management buyout or a sale to private-equity investors—so that its business is self-financing and its failure cannot affect the retail and commercial/wholesale banking units.*

---

* There is a question whether the separated corporate/wholesale and investment banks can continue to trade under, say, the Barclays name, or whether there must be a distinction at least to the extent that JPMorgan & Co. was split in the 1930s into today's JPMorgan and Morgan Stanley.

3. Scrapping the Bonus Pool and Capping Remuneration

This is tricky, but, in the end, I believe that there is no alternative to a remuneration cap. It is my belief that remuneration of employees at the retail and commercial/wholesale banks should be capped at an inflation-adjusted £200,000. This means that all existing bonus provisions must be suspended and, if there is to be a new bonus system, it must be implemented according to completely new guidelines.

The problem is that, despite the lessons of the banking crisis, the concept of the bonus pool lives on. It may not be so generous, and more of the bonus may be deferred or paid in shares, and it may be subject to "clawback" in later years—but the bonus still plays a big part in negotiations and performance assessments every year. It influences employees' behavior, and their attitude to senior management, to clients, to each other, and to the bank itself. Seen from outside, it is the curse of modern banking.

For years, bank executives have said they wished they could end this bonus-driven culture. But they have failed to do so for two main reasons: first, it gives them power; and, second, they are scared of losing what they call "talent." Over the past eight years, the one facet that regulators—and, of course, senior bankers—have not dared to change is the principle on which most dealmakers on Wall Street and in the City of London are hired: that they are mercenaries for some kind of licensed privateer. All well and good when the privateer is truly private; but no good at all when the institution is subsidized or underwritten by the state.

This is why revolutionizing pay needs an initiative from outside. Capping bonuses by itself is not good enough—especially when the cap is not defined in absolute terms, but only in relation to base salary. The remedy has to be to cap total remuneration and to abolish the bonus pool altogether at all banks that have access to the central bank's discount window. That would include all regulated retail and corporate/wholesale banks—but it would not catch investment banks or hedge funds *provided* they are set up as partnerships.

In my new banking world, any EU or third-country banks with subsidiaries in the UK, whose depositors might be protected by UK deposit insurance, must be subject to the same business split and the same remuneration cap as UK banks. I would even argue that EU banks that have "passported" branches into the UK should be subject to the same treatment—if this is possible according to EU law. And, if it isn't now, *it is something that Britain should demand as part of the renegotiation of its terms of EU membership.*

8

EIGHT FIRM STEPS

The main thrust of all these proposals is revolutionary: it is to simplify banks and to change their culture. If a government is to lead the rest of the developed world in banking reform, these are the steps that it needs to take:

1. Treat regulated banks for what they are: partially (in some cases, predominantly) state-sponsored institutions. In Britain's case, it should demonstrate this by fully nationalizing RBS and (possibly) Lloyds Banking Group.

2. Break up the systemically important banks, such as JP-Morgan Chase, Bank of America, Barclays, Deutsche Bank, BNP Paribas, and Credit Suisse, into three stand-alone entities—a retail bank and a corporate/wholesale bank (each of which should be separately capitalized) and an investment bank (which should be a partnership and must be economically independent of the former parent).

3. Ring-fence retail banking at other big banks such as Wells Fargo, Standard Chartered, and Commerzbank.

4. Put an absolute cap on remuneration at an inflation-adjusted $500,000 and abolish the bonus pool principle at all regulated banks, i.e., those that have access to the central bank's discount window.

5. Prohibit proprietary trading at corporate/wholesale banks, though they may offer clients prices in standard currency and interest-rate products. For more complex products, such banks may act for clients in an agency capacity only, procuring services from brokers, investment banks, hedge funds, or asset managers. And they may take only limited exposure to these counterparties in terms of credit and performance risk.

6. Force investment banks to restructure as partnerships—which would then be free to take risks as they please. Obviously, they would be governed by conduct-of-business rules and by stock-exchange regulation, but there would be no capital requirements. In this sense, they would be indistinguishable from hedge funds—and, indeed, they would trade among themselves, and with hedge funds and other sophisticated counterparties, in a very light regulatory environment.

7. Forbid the sale and purchase of credit derivatives by regulated banks—unless they have an offsetting position in the underlying credit.

8. Scrap the complex bank capital rules embodied in Basel II and III in favor of simplified standards for retail and corporate/wholesale banks—such as capital and liquidity ratios based on a percentage of overall assets. Moreover, a similar approach should be encouraged for systemically relevant financial institutions in the United States, Germany, France, and Switzerland.

9

MORE CLOUDS ON THE HORIZON

The Libor scandal—manipulation of the interest-rate benchmark by colluding traders—showed how vulnerable over-the-counter markets are to abuse. Result: six major banks were fined a total of $3.75 billion between 2012 and 2015. The foreign-exchange market scandal reinforced that view and led to another $6 billion of fines in 2014 and 2015. Likewise, in September 2015, twelve banks paid $1.9 billion to settle claims that they had manipulated the market in credit default swaps. It seems that when big banks get dealing in items that are not transparently quoted on a public exchange they will favor their own interests over the interests of the client. In theory, brokers are there to keep them honest. But in practice, brokers are often drawn into the web spun by the banks. That, anyway, is the contention of a class action filed in New York in November 2015 against ten big banks and two interdealer trading platforms, ICAP and Tradeweb, which handle over 50 percent of the $285 trillion of interest-rate swaps (75 percent of the total swap market) that are electronically traded. The suit claims that the banks acted as a cartel to deter their customers from dealing anonymously on other trading platforms.

This may seem arcane, but it adds fuel to a suspicion that no market traded bilaterally by banks is safe from manipulation by them, to the jeopardy of their clients. If it was true of Libor interest rates, foreign-exchange rates, and interest-rate swap prices, how about Eurobonds, municipal bonds, and the $12 trillion U.S. Treasury bill market? In November 2015 panelists at a futures industry conference in Chicago described the U.S. Treasury market as less transparent even than the swap market. Many trades are not reported and many are "internalized" by dealers (and thus not declared to the market), noted one panelist.

You could say that this is all in the nature of capitalism and we must live with it: dealers will always turn knowledge of deal-flow to their advantage; they take risks and should be duly rewarded.

Indeed, but when the rip-off is institutionalized and the risk run by the dealers is minimal, it's a different story. In the New York swaps case, the plaintiff accuses the ten big banks of "forcing buy-side investors to trade with them in an opaque and inefficient market in which the defendants hold all the cards."

The U.S. regulators, the Department of Justice, and Britain's Financial Conduct Authority have shown an appetite for pursuing such cases of market manipulation. They may go on to find abuse in other markets. But, given the tendency of a dozen or so of the world's biggest banks to cartel-like behavior, a better remedy would be to reduce their size and importance as quickly as possible. That certainly chimes in with the message of this book.

10

A PRACTICAL REVOLUTION

The motive behind these recommendations has been my growing unease, over the past fifteen years, with the way that "sophisticated" finance has developed into a self-referential, self-congratulating culture—voting itself rewards that are too high and, by implication, cannibalizing other parts of the economy. The financial industry has devoted itself overwhelmingly to self-serving innovations, and its utility (in all senses of the word) has been severely compromised.

Still, as I hope has been clear, I have no particular vendetta against millionaires or anyone who has made and enjoys their own wealth. Nor against those who by some fluke of regulation found that the rules worked in their favor and made them rich. But I am against those who believe, or who anyway maintain, that such flukes have added to the sum of human achievement and the general good. That includes apologists for the current state of affairs in banking and bank regulation.

In the United States, Britain, Germany, and other developed countries, we have seen banking systems evolve that are simply not efficient enough at serving the rest of the economy—and that impose a huge cost on the taxpayer when (as inevitably seems to happen) things go wrong. Attempts at reform have all too often been thwarted by the incumbents. And why not? In their place, I would probably do all I could to preserve my privileges—and the rent that I could extract as a result of them.

To me, that is all the more reason for a powerful force for change to come—from left or right field—and precipitate revolution. I am not a communist, an anarchist, or a hopeless romantic—but I am a revolutionary. What I've proposed in this book is a revolution in favor of the more efficient use of capital—in favor of a fairer distribution of the real costs and benefits of financial services. It is not a revolution against capitalism, but it does take for granted that the system we currently have in place is unsustainable—and must be transformed.

Glossary

The world of finance is not generally more complex or inscrutable than other industries, but more than most, it is enamored of its terminology. In this book, I've tried, as much as possible, to clarify and explain terms that may seem inscrutable, but the glossary that follows is a more comprehensive approach to the same problem. I hope it illustrates, above all, that obfuscation should be combatted in all realms of finance: including the linguistic.

AGENCY BONDS: Bonds sold by U.S. government-backed agencies whose debts are guaranteed by the U.S. government.

AGENCY PROBLEM: The temptation that those employed to run a company will put their interests ahead of those of the owners or customers.

ASSET-BACKED SECURITIES: Securities (see SECURITIES) that are linked to the value of an underlying asset, such as a portfolio of car loans, or credit-card receivables, or mortgages.

ASSET POOL: A selection of stocks, bonds loans, or other financial assets assembled to form the basis of asset-backed securities (see ASSET-BACKED SECURITIES).

BACK-TO-BACK LOAN: Precursor of the swap (see SWAP), whereby two borrowers agree to swap the proceeds of the loans and payments attached to loans raised in different currencies or different markets.

BAD BANK: When a bank is rescued or restructured, the unwanted and poorly performing assets are put in a "bad" bank to be run off or otherwise disposed of. The assets and businesses designated as worth keeping and developing are put in a "good" bank (see GOOD BANK).

BAILOUT: Rescue of a failing bank, usually with government money.

BANKING UNION: Proposed centralization of ultimate responsibility for bank oversight in the European Union (EU). The European Central Bank would supervise 130 or so of the banks in the euro area seen as systemic (see SYSTEMIC).

BASEL COMMITTEE ON BANKING SUPERVISION: An international committee of bank supervisors, originally from ten, now twenty-eight, major countries, which meets regularly to develop recommendations on bank supervision. Those recommendations have led to an increasingly complex series of rules, starting with Basel I in 1988, then Basel II in 1998 and Basel III, which is being phased in from 2013 to 2019.

BASEL III: The latest in a series of recommendations on bank capital requirements by the Basel Committee on Banking Supervision (see BASEL COMMITTEE).

BENCHMARK: A mutually agreed rate or value for an item that is regularly traded—such as the interbank lending rate (see LIBOR and INTERBANK).

BIG BANG: A landmark in 1986 when banks in Britain were for the first time allowed to buy brokers (see BROKER) and jobbers (see JOBBER) that dealt in stocks and bonds. British universal banking was born (see UNIVERSAL BANK).

BONUS: Extra pay to an employee, which is related to his performance or that of his department or the entire institution (often an automatic component of bankers' pay).

BONUS CAP: An upper limit on bonuses.

BONUS POOL: A share of bank revenues set aside as a source for paying bonuses.

BORROWING SECURITIES: Borrowing stocks and shares with a view to returning them at the end of the borrowing period. This is usually done in the expectation that the price will fall: the borrower sells the securities he has borrowed, hoping to buy them back in the market at a lower price (see also SHORT POSITION).

BROKER: A facilitator of financial or other transactions between two counterparties.

BROKER-DEALER: An institution licensed by the U.S. Securities & Exchange Commission to buy and sell securities and offer them to the public.

CAPITAL CHARGE: The amount of a bank's own funds (capital, contingent capital, and reserves) that a bank is expected by regulators to hold as a buffer against sudden credit or market shocks.

CASH MANAGEMENT: Handling the cash needs of a company or institution.

CDO, CLO: See COLLATERALIZED DEBT OBLIGATION and COLLATERALIZED LOAN OBLIGATION.

CDO MANAGER: An individual or a firm entrusted with buying and selling assets in the pool designed to back a CDO issue (see COLLATERALIZED DEBT OBLIGATION) to maintain performance— for instance by selling loans that might go bad.

CENTRAL BANK MONEY: Money created by a central bank simply by adding it as a balance-sheet item: the safest money there is, provided the country to which the central bank belongs does not go bust. Central bank money has been created recently to provide

quantitative easing to stimulate flagging economies (see QUANTI-
TATIVE EASING).

CHICAGO MERCANTILE EXCHANGE (CME): A commodities and futures exchange in Chicago. The first in the world to list financial
futures, starting with foreign currency contracts in seven currencies in 1972.

CLAWBACK: Canceling all or part of a bonus already awarded if
the recipient's or the company's performance turns out poorer
than expected.

CLEARING MEMBER: A trading member of an exchange that also
handles trades on behalf of clients, guaranteeing that the client
will fulfill its trading commitment.

COLLATERAL: An asset pledged by a borrower to a creditor as a
source of value in case he fails to perform on a contract.

COLLATERALIZED DEBT OBLIGATION (CDO): A security whose repayment is supported by an assortment of loans or bonds to different companies. The starting value of the asset pool is designed
to be greater than the value of the security, so that the excess value
in the loans or bonds can be used as collateral if some of the loans
go bad. For example 110 car loans totaling $1,100,000 are resold as
securities (1,000 pieces of paper, each with a face value of $1,000),
whose repayment depends on the performance of all those loans.
This means that even if a few of the loans go bad the holder of the
security still has a chance of making a profit.

COLLATERALIZED LOAN OBLIGATION (CLO): Used to describe a CDO (see CDO) if the debt is comprised of loans.

COMMERCIAL BANKING: Taking deposits and providing loans and simple financial services to big and small commercial clients.

COMMERCIAL PAPER: Short-term bonds sold by companies, repayable usually in one to six months.

COMPENSATION: A euphemism for pay (see also REMUNERATION).

COMPLIANCE: A part of the banking function that ensures that employees and procedures stick to the rules. Modern banks have a compliance department and compliance officers.

CONGLOMERATE: A collection of associated companies under the umbrella of one brand, or holding company (see HOLDING COMPANY).

CONTAGION: The effect on other financial institutions or markets if one of them falters.

CONTINGENT CAPITAL: Capital that is not common equity but a type of loan that converts into equity if the bank is in financial difficulty.

CoCos (CONTINGENT CAPITAL CONVERTIBLE SECURITIES): Bonds issued by banks that can be converted into equity if the bank's financial health falls below a specified trigger point.

CO-OPERATIVE BANK: A bank owned by all its members (see also MUTUAL BANK). An exception is Britain's Co-operative Bank, which now has a majority of private shareholders since its rescue in 2013.

CORPORATE ASSETS: Bonds or loans repayable by companies.

COUNTERPARTY: Person or entity on the other side of a transaction.

CRD 4: The European Union's Capital Requirements Directive 4. The latest in a series of EU bank regulations setting the amount of capital that banks should have relative to the risks on their balance sheet. These directives (CRDs 1–4) closely follow recommendations by the Basel Committee on Banking Supervision (see BASEL COMMITTEE). CRD 4 is roughly equivalent to Basel III (see BASEL III).

CREDIT BUREAU: A data company that tracks consumer borrowers' individual credit performance and provides potential lenders with a rough personal credit score.

CREDIT DEFAULT SWAP (CDS): A form of insurance against the event of a company defaulting on its debt. If there is a default event the insurer pays out and takes over the impaired debt. For example, an investor owning bonds issued by GlaxoSmithKline buys a CDS that will pay the value of those bonds in full if GSK defaults. In the event of a default the insurer (i.e., the provider of the CDS) pays the investor in full, then seeks to recover any residual value in the GSK bonds.

CREDIT DERIVATIVE: A generic term for any derivative (see DE-RIVATIVE) whose price depends on estimates of whether or not a credit, or bundle of credits, will be repaid in full.

CREDIT RATING AGENCY: An outfit that grades securities issued by companies and other entities according to the probability that they will go into default. The best known are Standard & Poor's, Moody's Investors Service, and Fitch Ratings.

CREDIT UNION: A club created to encourage personal savings and to lend those funds to local individuals and small businesses.

CROSS-FUNDING: The use of funds raised by one part of a financial group to finance another part of the same group.

CURRENCY SWAP: A swap agreement (see SWAP) based on the difference in cash flows between repayments of debt in two different currencies.

DEFAULT RISK: The risk that a borrower will fail to make timely payments on a debt.

DEFERRAL: Delaying payment of a bonus for a year or more to encourage longer-term behavior.

DEPOSIT INSURANCE: A scheme that guarantees bank depositors that their deposits (usually to a specified upper limit, such as $100,000) are safe, even if the bank fails.

DERIVATIVE: A financial product that derives its price from the variation in price of specified traded items, such as bonds, shares, or interest and currency rates.

DEVELOPMENT BANK: A bank, usually government-sponsored, that provides finance, usually medium-term loans, for projects and companies in sectors where the government(s) would like to encourage development.

DISCOUNT WINDOW: A facility offered by a central bank to authorized banks to ensure they have access to liquidity (see LIQUIDITY). It allows banks to raise short-term cash by pledging assets, usually government bonds, but also company shares and loans acceptable to the central bank. A discount is applied so that the borrower receives less cash than the full market value of the assets pledged.

DIVIDEND: A portion of company profits that is paid to shareholders, subject to approval at the shareholders' annual general meeting.

DODD-FRANK ACT (2010): An act passed in the United States in the aftermath of the financial crisis encompassing sweeping reforms of bank supervision and weaknesses in the mortgage market.

DOWNSIDE: The likely loss or other disadvantage that a deal might bring (see also UPSIDE).

EQUITY-FOR-DEBT SWAP: Whereby shares in a company are

swapped for bonds. Debt-for-equity swaps are more common, as a way of giving bondholders in a distressed company a chance of gain if the company recovers.

EUROPEAN SYSTEM OF CENTRAL BANKS: A network formed by all national central banks in the euro zone, with the European Central Bank (ECB) at its center. The national central banks act as agents of the ECB—i.e., since European monetary union in 1999 they have no longer acted as sovereign and independent central banks.

EURO ZONE: The group of countries that have the euro as their official currency.

EXPOSURE: Level of risk being run in a transaction or group of transactions, in a particular market, or with a particular counterparty (see COUNTERPARTY) or sector.

FEDERAL DEPOSIT INSURANCE CORPORATION (FDIC): A U.S. corporation that ensures that bank depositors with deposits up to $250,000 will be repaid in full. It is one of four major U.S. regulators of banking groups, the others being the Federal Reserve, the Securities & Exchange Commission, and the Office of the Comptroller of the Currency.

FILLING CUSTOMER ORDERS: Selling customers the assets they have asked for.

FINANCIAL ENGINEERING: Using financial skills to achieve often complex goals, such as matching a company's borrowing needs to its projected cash flows.

FINANCIAL TRANSACTION TAX: A tax applied to financial transactions either as a way to put a brake on trading volumes, or to bring in government revenue.

FIT-AND-PROPER PERSON: Someone regarded by the licensing authority as having sufficient integrity and competence to run a regulated financial institution.

FLOW MONSTER: Nickname given to a global investment bank that trades such large volumes of bonds, shares, and derivatives that it stands to benefit from economies of scale and timely information about trends in the market.

FRICTIONLESS: Used to describe trading that incurs zero or minimal transaction costs.

FRONT-RUN: To buy assets in anticipation that a client order will drive up the market price, then sell to the client or the market for a quick profit.

GAMING: Outsmarting rules in a way not intended by the rulemaker.

GLOBAL INVESTMENT BANK: One of a handful of banks that provide investment-banking services in all the world's main money centers.

GOOD BANK: A set of assets and businesses designated as worth keeping and developing when a bank is rescued or restructured. Unwanted and poorly performing assets, not needed in the "good" bank, are put in a "bad" bank to be run off or otherwise disposed of (see BAD BANK).

GRAMM-LEACH-BLILEY ACT (1999): U.S. legislation that allowed commercial banks to deal freely in securities and undertake other investment-banking activities, overturning the 1933 Glass-Steagall Act.

GUARANTEE: A promise to step in for the full amount of a contract if it is not honored.

HAIRCUT: The discount applied when assets are taken as collateral (see COLLATERAL), to ensure that the market value of the assets comfortably exceeds that of the cash advanced.

HEDGE: A financial position taken to reduce a perceived financial risk, such as a currency or interest-rate risk.

HEDGE FUND: A fund for professional investors that uses various financial techniques, including hedging unwanted risks (hence the name "hedge fund"), to aim for higher than average market returns.

HIGHLY RATED: Given a good credit rating by a rating agency (see RATING AGENCY).

HOLDING COMPANY: A company at the top of a hierarchy that owns stakes in other companies seen as part of the group, which is sometimes known as a conglomerate (see CONGLOMERATE).

HOUSING BUBBLE: A period during which house prices seem to be rising unstoppably, encouraging people to buy houses by borrowing beyond their means.

INFRASTRUCTURE FUND: An investment fund established to fund infrastructure projects, such as building roads, dams, and power stations.

INSTITUTIONAL INVESTOR: A general term applied to a body that invests funds professionally, such as an insurance company, pension fund, or other fund management company.

INSTRUMENT: Almost any item devised to have financial value.

INTERBANK: Refers to high-volume transactions between banks.

INTERCONNECTEDNESS: In finance, this refers to the huge number of bilateral arrangements running between banks active in money, lending, currency, and derivative markets. The failure of a single bank can lead to multiple disruptions of these arrangements and possibly the failure of other banks.

INTEREST-RATE SWAP: A swap agreement (see SWAP) based on two interest-rate flows, most usually between fixed-rate and floating-rate interest payments.

INTERNAL MODEL: A model (see MODEL) used for internal purposes by a bank to calculate the risk of the various assets on its balance sheet. Regulators under Basel II and Basel III rules (see BASEL III) allow sophisticated banks to use their internal models to calculate regulatory capital charges.

INVESTMENT BANKING: Banking that facilitates the issuing and trading of shares and bonds and the financing and financial restructuring of companies.

ISSUER OF SECURITIES: A company or other entity in whose name debt or equity securities are sold to raise money.

JOBBER: Until 1986, a short-term buyer and seller of securities to and from other dealers in the UK securities markets.

LANDESBANK: A regional German bank whose main job is to offer wholesale services to local savings banks and their customers. Many Landesbanken stepped outside this narrow brief in the 1980s in an attempt to rival global banks, with dire consequences. They are now trying to get back to their roots and prove that the basic model works.

LEAD-MANAGE: To be the bank chiefly responsible for organizing an issue of shares, bonds, or a syndicated loan (see SYNDICATED LOAN) for a company or other entity.

LEHMAN BROTHERS: An American investment bank that was

allowed to fail in September 2008—an event seen as a defining moment in the 2008 financial crisis.

LEVERAGE: The amount of assets or liabilities relative to the amount of capital held by a company or financial institution.

LEVERAGED LOAN: A loan that is many times larger than the capital base of the borrower. Leveraged loans are often used for acquisitions in which the buyer expects a rapid sale of part of the acquired assets to repay the leveraged loan.

LEVERAGE RATIO: The assets of a financial institution divided by its capital—a rough measure of how resilient the institution might be to shocks.

LIBOR (LONDON INTERBANK OFFERED RATE): An interest-rate benchmark determined by the average rate at which a group of banks in London offer to lend cash to each other short-term (between one and six months).

LIBOR SQUARED: Using the square of the Libor interest rate as the basis of a swap (see SWAP) to amplify the effect of a change in the Libor benchmark (making it more risky and volatile).

LIEN: The right to seize and sell an object, such as a house, to recover an unpaid claim on its owner (such as a mortgage).

LIQUIDITY: Access to ready cash. Banks must have a reserve of liquidity to meet sudden demands for cash by customers. A market provides liquidity if traders can buy and sell the assets, or other financial instruments quoted, easily, with a narrow difference between the buying and selling price.

LIQUIDITY BUFFER: A cushion of cash—or assets that can quickly be turned into cash—to protect an institution from financial shocks.

LIQUIDITY RESERVE: A level of liquidity (see LIQUIDITY) kept by banks to satisfy regulators and the market that they are solvent.

LIVING WILL: A published set of procedures whereby the businesses of a still solvent financial institution could be transferred or wound up with minimum damage to the rest of the financial system.

LOAN-TO-VALUE: The amount lent in a mortgage as a percentage of the estimated value of the property.

LONDON WHALE SCANDAL: Reference to a fiasco in 2012 when a small London-based department of U.S. investment bank JP-Morgan Chase lost an estimated $6.2 billion in trading synthetic credit derivatives.

MACRO-PRUDENTIAL: Overseeing the safety of the financial system on a big-picture basis.

MANAGEMENT BUYOUT: Acquisition of a company by its directors or other employees.

MARKET MAKING: Being ready, as a trading entity, to buy and sell to customers or other market participants at prices it has quoted in the market.

MASTER OF THE UNIVERSE: Term applied to high-flying investment bankers, or those who think they are.

MATURITY: The date, or length of time, by which a loan or bond must be repaid.

METRICS: Methods of calculation.

MITIGATE REGULATORY CAPITAL: Reduce the amount of capital that banks are required by regulators to maintain as a buffer against shocks.

MODEL: An attempt to formulate complex financial activity in simplified terms, in order to assign probability to different possible outcomes.

MORTGAGE-BACKED SECURITIES: See ASSET-BACKED SECURITIES.

MUTUAL BANK: A bank owned by its depositors or members (see also CO-OPERATIVE BANK).

NARROW BANK: A highly conservative banking model, whereby the bank takes deposits and safeguards the funds by investing them purely in risk-free government bonds.

NATIONAL CHAMPION: A company or bank that has global status and is thought to add to national prestige.

NOVATION: Rewriting one or more financial contracts with another party either to provide more clarity or to reduce complexity.

OFF BALANCE-SHEET: A financial engagement owned or controlled remotely so that its fluctuation in value does not affect the fortunes of the parent institution.

OFFSETTING CREDIT RISK: Reducing credit risk, for example by buying credit insurance that would compensate for losses if a company loan or bond is in default.

OLIGOPOLY: A market dominated by a handful of big firms.

PARTIAL GUARANTEE: A promise to step in for part of the amount if a contract is not honored.

PERSON-TO-PERSON LENDING: Lending whereby a private individual takes on the credit risk of loans to one or more persons.

POST COLLATERAL: To provide a lender with collateral for a loan or other obligation (see COLLATERAL).

PREFERENCE SHARES: Bonds with a coupon that depends on a company's financial performance. Under stress conditions the coupon may not be paid. In a restructuring or bankruptcy, preference shareholders rank higher than holders of common equity, who are the first class of investor to suffer loss, but lower than holders of senior debt.

PRIME BROKER: A provider, usually an investment bank, of financial and other services to hedge funds and private-equity firms.

PRIVATE-EQUITY FIRM: A firm that invests funds, usually gathered from professional investors, in minority or controlling stakes in companies, and which usually has a say in their management.

PRIVATE PLACEMENT: A loan or equity stake placed privately with selected investors rather than through a public offering.

PROFIT: Income generated by trading activity, minus costs.

PROPRIETARY TRADING: Taking speculative trading positions for a financial institution's own account.

PUBLICLY TRADED INSTRUMENT: A financial asset, such as a share, bond, or derivative standard enough to be traded on a stock exchange or electronic platform.

QUANTITATIVE EASING: The use of central bank money to buy assets from the market—usually government bonds—to stimulate a depressed economy.

QUANTITATIVE FINANCE: The use of sophisticated mathematics to steer financial trading decisions.

QUANTO SWAP: A currency swap agreement (see CURRENCY SWAP) in which the interest-rate indexes of the two currencies are switched. For example the yen side is determined by the prevailing dollar interest rate, and the dollar side by the yen rate.

RATING AGENCY: See CREDIT RATING AGENCY.

REAL ECONOMY, THE: Economic activity that is driven by manufacturing, production, or services other than financial services.

REFINANCE: To raise cash from a bank or central bank by pledging assets, such as shares, bonds, or property (see also COLLATERAL).

REMUNERATION: A euphemism for pay (see also COMPENSATION).

REPO: Short for repurchase agreement, which is an agreement to sell securities and buy them back after a certain period. Repos are a cheap way for owners of securities to raise short-term finance (see also SECURITIES LENDING).

RETAIL BANK: A bank that deals purely with consumers and small businesses.

REVENUE: Income generated by banking activity.

RING-FENCING: A separation so that a retail bank within a banking group has no financial relationship with other parts of the group.

RISK WEIGHT: A percentage grade applied to an asset according to its risk relative to that of a standard loan. For example, a bank loan to another bank may be graded as only 20 percent as risky as a loan to a commercial company; and a loan guaranteed by the state may be graded as having zero risk weight.

RISK-WEIGHTED ASSETS (RWAs): The total of a bank's assets after risk weights have been applied.

SAVINGS BANK: A retail bank usually owned by a municipality.

SECURITIES: Bonds and shares that are traded on a stock exchange or electronic platform, or bilaterally.

SECURITIZE: To divide the value of an asset, or bundle of assets, into tradable fragments that are sold to investors.

SHADOW BANK: Entity outside the regulated banking system that nevertheless performs some banking functions, such as making loans and using leverage (see LEVERAGE) to make investments. The broadest definition of *shadow bank* includes hedge funds, investment managers, and private equity firms.

SHORT POSITION: An obligation to deliver a commodity or financial asset by a certain date. Often used by dealers who are betting that the price will go down. They create a short position by borrowing or selling, say, gold or shares, promising to deliver them at a future date. If the price has indeed gone down they can find them more cheaply in the market and make a profit. If the price goes up they make a loss (see also BORROWING SECURITIES).

SHORT-TERMISM: The inclination to aim financial decisions at short-term results rather than longer-term success.

SINGLE RESOLUTION MECHANISM (SRM): A procedure that would set up an emergency euro-zone fund intended to help wind up any failing systemic bank (see SYSTEMIC).

SINGLE RULEBOOK: An attempt to draw up a harmonized set of banking rules for the European Union, a task given to the London-based European Banking Authority (EBA).

SINGLE SUPERVISORY MECHANISM (SSM): A procedure for centralized bank supervision in the euro zone, and other non-euro-zone states that elect to join the SSM.

SOVEREIGN RATING: The credit rating of a sovereign country based on the likelihood that it will make full and timely payments of its debts.

SPECIAL PURPOSE VEHICLE (SPV): An entity devised to hold specific assets for a financial institution, remotely enough so that failure of those assets, in theory, does not affect the institution.

SPREAD: The difference between one market price and another, for instance in the buying and selling price of a security.

STANDARDIZED MODEL: A method prescribed by bank regulators for calculating the amount of regulatory capital to be held against various classes of risk exposure. Regulators allow more sophisticated banks to use an internal model for the same purpose (see INTERNAL MODEL).

STICKY: Refers to bank deposits that, because of customer loyalty or inertia, are unlikely to be withdrawn suddenly, or indeed ever.

STOCKBROKER: An arranger of trades in shares and bonds and other financial instruments between counterparties (see also BROKER).

STOCKJOBBER: An intermediate buyer and seller of stocks and bonds who helps to provide a market with liquidity (see also JOBBER).

STRUCTURED PRODUCT: General term for assets or derivatives bundled together by an investment bank for sale to investors.

SUBORDINATED DEBT: Debt that ranks below senior debt in bankruptcy or restructuring proceedings. (See also PREFERENCE SHARES, CONTINGENT CAPITAL, and CoCos).

SWAP: An agreement to exchange the difference between two sets of cash flows on a notional principal amount (for example, $100 million), which may be calculated on the basis of different interest or currency rates, or any other type of index.

SYNDICATED LOAN: A multimillion-dollar loan arranged among a syndicate of lenders, whereby each lends a part of the total.

SYSTEMIC: Refers to a financial institution big and interconnected enough to affect the financial system and the economy in general if it gets into trouble (see also INTERCONNECTEDNESS).

SYSTEMICALLY RELEVANT BANK: See SYSTEMIC.

TAX BREAK: Favorable tax treatment given by a government to certain kinds of business to encourage their development.

TEAR-UP: Cancellation of one or more contracts with another party to reduce complexity.

TOO BIG TO FAIL: Used to describe a financial institution so important to national or international financial stability that its home government would be bound to rescue it if it were threatened with failure.

TRADE AT A DISCOUNT: Bonds or other types of obligations being valued by the market at less than 100 percent of their face value, reflecting the risk that they might not be repaid in full.

TRADE FINANCE: Provision of short-term loans to a company to finance a specific export or import.

TRADING EXPOSURE: Open-ended risk run by institutions engaged in proprietary trading or market making (see MARKET MAKING, PROPRIETARY TRADING, and EXPOSURE).

TRADING RISK: Ultimately all financial trading can be seen as exchanging one kind of risk for another: hence as the trading of risk.

TRANCHE: A slice of an investment that is priced or sold separately.

TREASURY BONDS: Bonds issued by the U.S. government.

TURNOVER: The number of times an asset is replaced during a given period.

UNDERLYING CREDIT: The actual determinant of credit performance (i.e., the actual credit name) used as a reference for a credit derivative.

UNDERWRITING: Guaranteeing a minimum price for a new issue of shares and bonds.

UNDERWRITING POSITION: The financial risk involved in underwriting a share or bond issue (see UNDERWRITING).

UNIVERSAL BANK: A bank that provides all types of financial services to a wide spectrum of customers from the man in the street to governments and industrial companies.

UNLIMITED LIABILITY: Personal responsibility for all commercial losses of an enterprise.

UPSIDE: The likely profit or other advantage that a deal might bring (see also DOWNSIDE).

VOLCKER RULE: A part of the Dodd-Frank Act of 2010 passed in the United States in the aftermath of the financial crisis (see DODD-FRANK ACT). The Volcker Rule bars big banks from proprietary trading (see PROPRIETARY TRADING) or investing their capital in shadow banks (see SHADOW BANKS) such as private equity firms (see PRIVATE EQUITY FIRMS) and hedge funds (see HEDGE FUNDS).

WAR-GAMING: Enaction by participants of a simulated crisis or other scenario to gain some less costly experience of the real thing.

WINDUP PROCESS: Procedure for closing down a financial institution aimed at causing the least possible mess (see also LIVING WILL).

WRITE: To be the risk-bearer in an insurance or option contract. A writer of a credit default swap (see CREDIT DEFAULT SWAP) bears the risk that the credit in question will default.

ZERO RISK WEIGHT: See RISK WEIGHT.

Acknowledgments

The ideas in this book were first presented as a discussion paper at a round table organized by the Centre for the Study of Financial Innovation (CSFI). My thanks to Andrew Hilton, director of the CSFI, for the airtime and some helpful editing. Thanks also to David Green at Civitas, Benedikt Fehr and Thomas Mayer in Frankfurt, Matthew Rose in Berlin, Beat Wittman in Zurich, and David Clark in Luxembourg for helping to give the ideas a wider airing; and to many friends for their encouragement, especially Will Facey, now at Medina Publishing, who first urged me to publish my thoughts in book form, and Mark Krotov at Melville House for picking up the baton.

About the Author

David Shirreff has been reporting on finance since the early 1980s. In 1987, he cofounded *Risk* magazine. From 2001 to 2014, he worked for the *Economist* in London, Frankfurt, and Berlin reporting on many aspects of business, finance, and the European monetary union. He is the author of *Dealing with Financial Risk*, in the *Economist*'s series of business books.